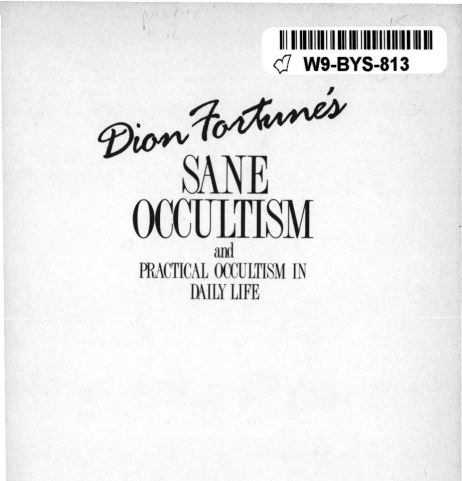

Dion Fortune's

SANE
OCCULTISM

and

PRACTICAL OCCULTISM IN
DAILY LIFE

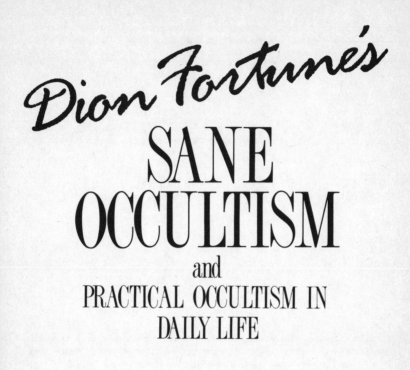

Dion Fortune's
SANE OCCULTISM
and
PRACTICAL OCCULTISM IN DAILY LIFE

THE AQUARIAN PRESS
Wellingborough, Northamptonshire

This edition first published 1987

British Library Cataloguing in Publication Data

Fortune, Dion
[Sane occultism]. Dion Fortune's Sane
occultism; and, Practical occultism in
daily life.
1. Occult sciences
Rn: Violet Mary Firth I. [Sane occultism]
II. Title III. Fortune, Dion. Practical
occultism in daily life
133   BF1411

ISBN 0-85030-663-9

*The Aquarian Press is part of the
Thorsons Publishing Group*

Printed and bound in Great Britain

2 4 6 8 10 9 7 5 3 1

Contents

The works of the late Dion Fortune were written a long time ago and since then a great deal more has been understood and realized so that many of the ideas then expressed are not now necessarily acceptable. Also, much of what she wrote was written from the viewpoint of the psychic. Psychism is simply one type of inner awareness and there are other types at least as valid and as common. Non-psychic readers, therefore, can translate experience in terms of psychic imagery into terms of their own inner awareness.

The publication of these books continues at present because there is still much of value in them and because they act as valuable pointers to seekers.

Details of the aims and work of the Society of the Inner Light, founded by Dion Fortune, may be obtained by writing (with postage please) to the Secretary at 38 Steele's Road, London NW3 4RG, England.

In December 1942 Dion Fortune wrote:

There are things I wrote of *Spiritualism* twenty years ago which, in the light of wider experience, I would not write today, and to cite these as evidence against me is to deny the possibility of human progress.

PART ONE
SANE OCCULTISM

1.

What is Occultism?

Very few of those who are interested in occultism pause to ask themselves what occultism really is. They may know that the word 'occult' means hidden, and that 'esoteric', which is often used as its synonym, means 'for the few'. If they put the two together, they may conclude, and rightly, that occult science is really a branch of knowledge which is hidden from the many and reserved for the few.

An immense mass of verbiage has gathered around the Sacred Science since Mme Blavatsky drew back the curtain of the Sanctuary, and the Theosophical Society, to popularize the ancient Mystery-teaching. Imagination, freed from the bonds of proof, has had free rein, and scoffers have found ample material that was legitimate game for their comments.

The pseudo-occultism of the present day, with its dubious psychism, wild theorizing, and evidence that cannot stand up to the most cursory examination, is but the detritus which accumulates around the base of the Mount of Vision. All such worthless rubbish is not worth the powder and shot of argument; in order to form a just estimate of the Sacred Science we must study originals, and try to penetrate the minds of the great mystics and *illuminati* whose works bear evidence of first-hand knowledge of the supersensible worlds.

Leaving aside all theories and dogmatic teaching, we find a consensus of agreement on certain matters of experience. There are states of consciousness which transcend the normal, and when these states prevail, we can discern forms of existence with which normally we have no contact. All the seers are agreed on this point, and we may take it as being the fundamental experience from which occult science is derived. There are universal traditions concerning superhuman beings who taught occult science to the remote ancestors of the races and founded their civilization; these statements, however, being unverifiable according to the accepted rules of evidence, will be put aside for the purpose of the present discussion.

Let us then concede, as we cannot very well deny in face of the available evidence, that the supernormal faculties of the human mind open up to man a supernatural range of experience. It is the cumulative supernatural experience of the ages, perceived by means of the supernormal faculties sporadically developed in mankind, that forms the subject-matter of occult science and the data for its speculations.

It is the sporadic development of the supernormal faculties, however, that makes evidential proof a difficulty.

Natural science lays its evidence before the five physical senses possessed by every normal human being; occult science makes its appeal to the judgment of senses but rarely to be found developed in human beings. The average man has to base his opinion in occult matters upon circumstantial evidence. Occult science, like classical music, reserves itself for the few whose training and natural gifts enable them to appreciate it. The Philistine is unapproachable because there is no common standpoint from which a start can be made.

In these latter days, however, there is a widespread occurrence of minor degrees of psychism. Many people have had experiences which have set them thinking and asking questions. They have glimpsed something outside the four walls of our everyday life, and they are no longer contented with the statement that nothing exists save that which we habitually see.

In their quest they may follow the line of experimental research, as the spiritualists have done; unearthing in the course of their work a vast mass of phenomena of the supersensible states of existence. Or, following another line of advance, they may ask their questions of those who go to tradition for their explanation.

Until one studies the literature of the subject, one is utterly unaware of its extent; it reaches from the oral traditions on the one hand, through the mythologies developed and systematized in the ancient literatures, to the writings of highly trained philosophers whose speculations led them 'beyond our bourne of time and space.'

It must, however, always be kept in mind that occultism is more than a philosophy of science: it is a vast range of experience, and it is this body of experience that its speculations seek to systematize and explain.

We can define occultism as an extension of psychology, for it studies certain little-known aspects of the human mind and the mind side of Nature. Its findings, rightly formulated and understood, fit in with what is already established in psychology and natural science. This mutual corroboration must be the test of occult science. There must be no discrepancies between its findings and those of natural science upon such points as natural science is in a position to test.

We must no longer content ourselves with wild statements of psychic experiences in proof of which no shadow of independent evidence can be offered. We must realize that if we are dealing with genuine phenomena, they will bear investigation. In seeking to investigate these little-known aspects of the mind, let us remember that they have their technique, and unless we are prepared to observe that technique we will no more obtain accurate results than we should if the object of our study were bacteriology.

Occultism, however, is more than a science to be pursued objectively; it provides also a philosophy of life derived from its experiences, and it is this philosophical, or even religious aspect, that attracts most of those who devote their lives to it. Out of experience of the rare states of consciousness which it studies comes a greatly changed attitude towards revealed religion, for the seeker has now penetrated to the planes whence the revelations come, and for him they have an entirely different significance and validity. He is no longer dependent upon faith, he has had personal experience, and out of that experience he tends to formulate a religious belief in which he himself aspires to share in the work usually assigned to saints and angels as the ministers and messengers of God. From time immemorial the training and teaching of specially selected individuals have gone on with that end in view, and the schools dedicated to that work are known as the Mystery Schools.

Experience of the rarer forms of natural phenomena brings the conviction that their influences in a subtle and little-understood fashion, affect normal human life very much more than is realized, especially in the spheres of disease and therapeutics.

But in addition to their teaching concerning the nature of the invisible planes of existence, the Mystery Schools teach the great fundamental doctrine of reincarnation, that is to say, the oscillation of the soul between the seen and the Unseen. This is a concept which changes our entire attitude towards life, and on this point occultism has not only a philosophy, but a system of ethics.

To the man or woman dissatisfied with the conventional explanations of a philosophy and a science limited to the evidence of the five physical senses, occultism opens a rich vein of ore to be had for the working. Its speculations throw light upon every aspect of life; they explain much that, considered only from the mundane aspect, is inexplicable, and they place religion upon a basis of experience, not of blind belief.

Those are the gifts that are available for men through the opening of the Mysteries; an opening which has been going on for the last fifty years, till now the doors stand wide and beams of light shine out from within.

2.

Is Occultism Worth While?

Whatever path in life a man may have chosen for himself or have had forced upon him, there comes a time when he looks back and asks himself whether it has all been worth while, when he looks ahead and asks himself whether it is right to go on or had he better say 'Mea culpa' and retrace his steps? The more sincere he is, the more faithful he is to the highest he knows, the oftener will come the heart-searching which is the highest tribute to Truth, a tribute infinitely higher than belief or sacrifice. It has nothing in common with the wavering which is the product of a lack of stamina, nor the abandonment of principles which comes in the absence of real convictions; it is not the product of weakness, but of strength, a strength that

'Can make one heap of all its winnings,
And stake it on one turn of pitch and toss'

of an integrity which really believes that 'There is no religion higher than Truth' and is prepared to face martyrdom for it, even that hardest of martyrdoms which is received in the house of one's friends.

That which remains after such an acid test of intellectual honesty may indeed be ranked as pure gold, and it is such gold, bought at such a price, that is the standard of value for our human life on this globe: by it every attainment and revelation must be tested in our limited and relative world. It is the Word made flesh among us.

Those of us who have chosen the Path of Occultism are even more in need of self-criticism than most people, for we have chosen for our study a subject in which there is no standard of criticism and in which each is a law unto himself, claiming, if he be so minded, independent revelation from sources beyond the judgment of human reason—a possession as unsatisfactory as a private printing-press for bank-notes.

We know that revelations, or, more truly, realizations, come to human consciousness, just as we know that bank-notes are legal tender, but we must never forget that revelations and bank-notes further resemble each other in that they have no value unless they represent actualities. For a bank-note to have value it must be redeemable in gold at any moment. For a revelation to have value it must be valid in a spiritual crisis.

Self-questionings are like a trial balance which enables the banker to estimate his solvency. He does not wait for a run on the bank to prove whether his gold reserve is equal to his note issue.

The revelations, the secret traditional wisdom that never gets tested by impartial criticism, the unknown powers, all the mystery and imaginings that constitute occult science, badly need such a periodical trial balance if they are to maintain any semblance of solvency.

When we look back upon the history of occult science, the outlook is not encouraging. Why is it that occultism has produced such a crop of charlatans and few, if any, intellects of the first water?

The grandeur of its theories ennobles human life and enables us to see our fate and acts in a perspective related to the cosmos; but is that glorious background interstellar space or painted canvas?

There is only one test, to walk straight up to it and see whether the stones of the Path are beneath one's feet or if one has simply torn one's way into the sordid back premises of a theatre.

Speaking for myself, I essayed that experiment upon my first introduction to occult science. In brilliant colours, books, lectures, and personal talks depicted occult arts and astral phenomena and a cosmogony of the type of the elephant who stood upon a tortoise, and I saw at the first glance that I was dealing with painted cloth and put my foot through it to show my opinion of it.

Then I used my knowledge of psychology to enable me to go behind the scenes and penetrate into the minds and motives of those who were staging the puppet-show I had been invited to witness. I saw the wires that supported the fairies and the machine that enabled the god to appear at the critical moment; the manager with one eye on the box office, the author with a much-revised manuscript; the producer in consultation with the stage-carpenter and limelight man; the actors trying to synthesize their egos and their parts.

Then I penetrated deeper behind the scenes of the theatre; I saw the different esoteric schools as dressing-rooms in which the actors made up for their parts; I discovered the dirty and draughty stone stairway by which they entered the theatre, and I descended it; I issued forth by the stage door into the sordid purlieus of theatre-land where men and women fought outside gin-palaces and children sprawled in the dirt of the gutter, and there, lifting my eyes for relief from the sordidness of it all, I saw above me the very stars in their remote and shining reality that had been depicted upon the painted scenery of the theatre.

Then, and then only, did I see the significance of the drama and realize that it was not an attempt to *deceive* but to *portray*, and I was glad to go in humility and gratitude to the front entrance and pay the price of a seat that I might watch the interpretation of life that was being represented therein. I had had my lesson and learnt the function and limitation of a school of initiation.

We have to distinguish between the symbolic expression of abstract ideas and the actual delineation of concrete objects. It is said of the Mysteries that the candidate was led on from degree to degree and shown more and more recondite symbols of the Godhead, and at the end, when the final curtain was drawn aside, was revealed to him an empty shrine and a voice whispered in his ear, 'There is no God.'

Whoever has penetrated behind the drop-scene, which is also the Veil of the Temple, knows this to be true. There is no God of Israel to fight for him in battle and snuff up the savour of burnt offerings, but— there is a Logos, and the nature of the Logos can only be apprehended by those who can meditate in an empty shrine, that is to say, can think without a symbol. The training of the degrees is designed to teach the mind to rise to the abstract and transcend thought, for it is only when thought ceases that apprehension begins.

No one can teach occult science who is not able to draw aside the curtain and reveal the empty shrine, who does not know that the occult doctrines are a system of algebra that enables the mind to function beyond the range of thought. Whoever thinks that the Planes and the Rays and the Hierarchy exist in time and space is not an initiate and therefore cannot be an initiator.

The difference between the occultaster and the occultist is that the former believes that the innermost shrine contains the god, and the latter knows that the God is within him. The former believes in revelation and the latter in realization. The former believes in a special message to himself from his Master, a special mandate from Heaven; the latter knows that in God we live and move and have our being. The former believes in the astral plane as objective reality; the latter knows it to be objective imagination.

This does not mean, however, that the astral plane is non-existent, but it *does* mean that it is the psychology of the objective imagination which is the true study of the practical occultist.

This brings us back to the point from which we started. Is occultism worth while? It is just as much and as little worth as mathematics, to which it is precisely analogous. The mathematician neither bakes a loaf nor digs a field, but his science is the fundamental basis of knowledge to whose terms all things must be reduced for final and accurate expression. What mathematics are to matter and force, occult science is to life and consciousness; there is possible no final expression or synthesis without the use of its peculiar methods. Therefore I maintain that it is worth while, and am satisifed that the time I have spent in its pursuit has not been wasted.

But, on the other hand, I maintain that some occult systems I have met with are not worth while. Though an initiatory system may justly be likened to a theatre, the teaching it conveys may not only be likened to such a play as *Hamlet*, but to such another as *Sweeny Todd, the Demon Barber of Fleet Street*. People who would sit enthralled through one of these plays would walk out in the first act of the other. Ninety per cent of the books on occultism are conceived in the spirit and written in the manner of the comic strip; they offend the taste of any educated person. As long as the occult doctrines are presented in such a guise they can never command the respect of those whose respect is worth having. There must always, it is true, be milk for babes and strong meat for strong men, but there is no need to accept silliness for simplicity, or intellectual confusion for profound wisdom. Large chunks of unverified and unverifiable statements and a thick treacly smear of sentimental humanitarianism are the mixture from which all too many esoteric books are compounded, and they make one ashamed to call oneself an occultist. Such a book as *The Ancient Wisdom* commands respect as a literary production even from those who do not accept its conclusions, but some of the utterances that have been given to the world in the name of Occult Science are simply in execrable taste and would disgrace a patent medicine.

We must remember that the Sacred Science only exists on this plane in the consciousness of its studènts; cosmic law and occult doctrine, as we know them, are only human conceptions of that which transcends any powers of direct perception possessed by the incarnated ego, and can be no more than an approximation, an attempt to conceive with the aid of a symbol that which in itself is unthinkable.

There is no Royal Road to initiation, but only the path worn by many wandering feet. Up this we must struggle as best we may with for our guide none other than our highest realization, and if the light that is in us be darkness, how great is that darkness? An order or fraternity upon the physical plane is what we make it; the Masters upon the astral planes are what we conceive them to be. It is only through human consciousness that Spirit can work upon the plane of matter. The astral plane is simply thought into existence and thought out of existence by the composite imagination of the globe, and we are freed from its dominion when we realize its subjective nature.

Occult science, rightly understood, teaches us to regard all things as states of consciousness, and then shows us how to gain control of consciousness subjectively; which control, once acquired, is soon reflected objectively. By means of this conscious control we are able to manipulate the plane of the human mind. It is a power that is neither good nor evil in itself but only as it is used. The initiate of the Right-hand Path, dedicated to the service of God, conceives that it should be used solely for the purpose of bringing human consciousness to an awareness of God in all that that implies when understood in its fullest significance. He uses his knowledge of the mind to make it the instrument of the Spirit, in contradistinction to the initiate of the Left-hand Path, who uses his knowledge of the mind to make it the servant of his passions. Occultism can never be an end in itself nor a mere satisfaction of intellectual curiosity, but the most potent weapon in the hands of the intellect. Is it worth while for men of goodwill to learn to handle this terrible two-edged sword? It is not only worth while, but essential for the safety of the race, for so many men of ill-will have learnt to handle it.

When one sees what can be done by the misuse of the knowledge of the hidden side of things, one feels that no sacrifice is too great, no risk too dangerous, to enable one to stand in the breach between the Powers of Darkness and their innocent victims. Therefore it is that there will always be found souls who will think it worth while to make the Great Sacrifice which is Initiation, and to offer the dedication of the self to the service of the Powers of Light in order that these Powers may be able to manifest on the planes of form through the channel which the human consciousness can open to them.

3.

The Deeper Issues of Occultism

What is occultism? This is a question we may very well ask if we intend to devote time and trouble to its pursuit. Are we to content ourselves with tales of haunted houses, accounts of telepathy among primitive peoples, and research into the esoteric literature of the past? These things certainly have their value; all available occult phenomena should be carefully investigated, not only for the sake of obtaining knowledge, but also for the sake of unmasking charlatans, and the results obtained by investigators in the past are of the greatest value for counterchecking the results we are obtaining at the present day.

But is this enough? Is our attitude towards occult science to be the same as our attitude towards the classical languages, in which we admire the masterpieces of antiquity but ourselves produce no living literature in the present? We know that the Mysteries exercised a profound influence on the ancient civilizations, and that some of the noblest men of all races were inspired by them and regarded them with reverence and awe. Are the phenomena we call occult merely those of the seance room on a larger scale, or, in addition to the little-known laws of Nature whose operations we seek to penetrate, is there an energizing spiritual influence such as raised the consciousness of the initiates of old and gave them a deeper understanding of their gods?

Let us consider the phenomena which may justly be described as occult, or hidden in their working and nature. Ectoplasm, psychometry, clairvoyance in all its forms, telepathy, the various forms of divination, which are far from being altogether delusive, mystic experiences, conversion, trance and rapture; hypnotism, suggestion, and auto-suggestion, the survival of bodily death, and last, but not least, certain forms of mental disease—all these things are hidden in their nature, not amenable to ordinary scientific methods of investigation with instruments of precision, and legitimately form the field of investigation of occult science.

There is, however, another aspect to occult science as well as its scientific side, and that is the realm of inner experience which its practical application as an art opens up. The gateway into the Unseen can be found by the practical application of its principles, and those who care to fulfil the conditions and take the risk may adventure therein. The powers that the ancient rituals invoked still remain and are not very far to seek for those who combine knowledge, faith, and courage.

If, however, we desire to essay this adventure, we should remember that the ancient rituals were used as part of a religious system, and that no initiate of the ancient Mystery Schools would ever have dreamed of experimenting with them to satisfy his curiosity or love of the marvellous: he approached them with reverence after strict discipline of character and severe tests of fitness. It was when the lofty ideals fell into abeyance that phallicism and black magic began.

If we want to penetrate into deeper issues of occultism it is not enough that we should approach it out of intellectual curiosity; this will reveal us no more than its outer form. The Occult Path is not so much a subject of study as a way of life. Unless the element of devotion and sacrifice be present, the key will not turn in the lock that opens the door of the Mysteries. Unless we approach the Sacred Science as did the initiates of old, we shall not find in it what they found. It is not enough that we work for its secrets as men work for the prizes of their profession; we must live for it as men live for a spiritual idea. There is only one motive that will take us safely through the labyrinth of astral experience—the desire for light on the path of spiritual development that ends in Divine Union. This was the goal of the Mysteries in their noblest form, and it is only by seeking the same goal that we shall be able to enter into them in their higher aspect. Occult science is a very potent thing, and many people are protected in their researches therein by their own ineptitude; did they succeed in some of the operations they undertake, their natures, unpurified and undisciplined, would be shattered by the result. It is only because no power comes through that no disaster follows. If we desire safely to investigate the Mysteries, we must first approach them under their nobler aspect as part of a system of spiritual regeneration, and only after we have submitted to their discipline and offered the dedication of the lower self to the purposes of the higher, *and had that dedication accepted*, can we safely study the magical aspects of occultism which usually attract the unenlightened.

Our intellectual questionings can only find their resolution in spiritual illumination. Occult science, rightly understood, is the link between psychology and religion; it gives the means of a spiritual approach to science, and a scientific approach to the spiritual life. The experiences to which it admits us, rightly understood, form a stairway from rational brain-consciousness, dependent on the five physical senses, to the direct apprehensions of spiritual intuition. Occultism can never be an end in itself, it does but open up a wider horizon that ever recedes as we approach it; we are still in the realms of appearance. Nevertheless it can be an invaluable means to many ends. A knowledge of its philosophy can give a clue to the researches of the scientist and balance to the ecstasies of the mystic; it may very well be that in the possibilities of ritual magic we shall find an invaluable therapeutic agent for use in certain forms of mental disease; psychoanalysis has demonstrated that these have no physiological cause, but it can very seldom effect a cure. It is here that the occultist with his knowledge of the hidden side of things can teach the psychologist a very great deal.

Occultism is a Sacred Science and should be approached with reverence. Straight is the gate and narrow the way that leads to its holy places and few there be that find it; The Angel with the Flaming Sword still guards the gate of the Mysteries, and it is not wise to expose our souls to that force until we have purified them and are sure that we can give the right pass-word when it is demanded of us.

There comes a time in the experience of every student of occult subjects, provided he is sufficiently interested in them, when the ideas that occupy his mind begin to affect him; and the Unseen World of which he has read is slowly rising above the horizon of consciousness and the subtle is becoming tangible. He will find himself in a veritable No Man's Land of the mind, and he must do one of two things, and do it quickly. He must either bolt back into his body like a rabbit down its hole, or he must press on and open up the higher consciousness. But one thing he must not do, he must not linger in the land of phantasms that is the frontier between the subconsciousenss and superconsciousness, for that way lies madness.

When he comes to the gate of the higher consciousness, however, he will be met by the Angel of the Threshold who will ask him the age-old question that he must answer before he can pass on, and the answer to this question is not any Shibboleth that admits to a secret society, but the very reasonable query to be addressed to the stranger who knocks at any door, 'What is it you want?' and the answer to that question will depend, not on the knowledge, but on the character of the applicant.

If rightly answered, the way will be made plain for his advancement, and if wrongly answered, he will be left to find his way back to the earth-plane as best he may, and that is neither a very pleasant nor a very safe experience.

To study occultism is to connect oneself up with a great power-house in the Unseen. There may be no tangible results because one's nature is made of non-conducting material, or because doubt of the reality of the phenomena investigated prevents the terminals of the psychic contact from being pushed home in their sockets. Knowledge and Force form the two arcs of the circuit, and when these are conjoined the power flows through. A nature which contains no force can study the Sacred Science and no results will be brought about, and a nature which has no knowledge will be unable to utilize its force; but where there is both knowledge and force it is only a matter of time till some illuminative idea gives a sudden glimpse of the significance of the inner life which completes the contact, and that person, for good or evil, is in circuit with the unseen power-house. For occult science, in itself, is neither good nor evil save as it is used, and that is why it is so necessary to approach it with clean hands, a pure heart, and a disciplined and dedicated will.

Occultism is not child's play, and it is very far from being fool-proof; for its pursuit strength is required as well as purity; but all who have touched its deeper issues unite in declaring that it is no will-o'the-wisp, dancing over a bottomless bog, but a true path to the Light, though narrow as a razor's edge.

4.

Credulity in Occult Research

Occult science has two enemies to contend with—the sceptical materialist who denies everything, and the credulous occultaster who believes everything. Serious students need to find the Middle Way between these two extremes; they must, on the one hand, avoid credulity, and on the other, recognize that the nature of proof available concerning the Inner Planes differs from that available for natural science.

Spiritualism, working up from the material plane through the denser strata of the Unseen, has been able to make use of a technique which satisfies even the laboratory-trained orthodox scientist; but the occultist, working in less tangible spheres, cannot avail himself of instruments of precision, and appears to have given up as hopeless any attempt at proof, satisfied if he attains to personal certainty.

This is an unsatisfactory state of affairs, and opens wide the door to charlatanism and delusion, and we need to be quite sure that it is inevitable before we acquiesce. It is my contention that we need not rest satisfied with so insecure a position, for there are ways of testing the findings of clairvoyant investigation that will enable us to assess their value without spoiling the experiment.

There are many different kinds of occult experiments, and I do not here propose to consider all that ground which has been adequately explored by the workers in psychic research; nor yet the poltergeist type of phenomena wherein the evidence of non-psychic witnesses has to be investigated, for both these are amenable to the ordinary laws of proof; but rather to consider the type of psychic research by clairvoyant vision with which the work of Rudolf Steiner and C. W. Leadbeater has made us familiar. It is very necesary that we should have some criterion for judging this type of work, for hosts of psychics have sprung up who lay claim to psychic vision, and declare that they see people's auras, read their past incarnations, or can conduct investigations of the Akashic Records and the astral plane, and offer no proof beyond their word.

There is, let us admit it, substantial evidence that all these things can be done, but there is not always substantial evidence that a particular psychic is doing them; but we need to remember that because we discount the findings of a particular psychic, we are not disproving psychism, nor are we even discrediting that psychic, for no one knows better the extreme delicacy of their gift and its liability to distortion than those who themselves have vision.

In dealing with occult experiments we need to adopt two attitudes and to keep them distinct. At the time of the experiment we must have absolute faith, and after the experiment is over we must be impartially critical towards its results. Faith is necessary at the time of the experiment, because suspicion or scepticism gives unconscious suggestion to the medium or experimenter; and as those engaged in using the supernormal faculties are always in a very sensitive condition, a sceptical attitude on the part of an experimenter may effectually prevent the carrying out of an experiment by upsetting the psychic, making him lose his self-confidence and doubt himself, whereupon his faculties automatically close down; he fumbles tentatively on the borderland of his own subconscious mind and fails to pass out into the higher consciousness. Those who take part in any occult investigation should make up their minds to accept the theories on which it is based as working hypotheses, and to give themselves up whole-heartedly to the experiment, while it is in progress. In this way, the group-mind of the circle gives subconscious suggestion to the psychic and helps him to rise to a higher plane. Once he is safely established there, his confident and awakened consciousness tends to pull his circle up after him; they, too, become at least partially aware of the presence of the Unseen, and their roused emotion and confidence lift their psychic up yet higher, and he becomes able to give them something worth having. None of the higher types of psychic faculty can be exercised unless the circle has also raised its consciousness a plane.

This attitude, however, should be reserved solely for the occasion of the experiment. As soon as it is completed, the experimenter should become a scientist again, and examine his results in the cold light of science. His judicial attitude, however, should not be that of the English Law, which has only two verdicts, 'Guilty or not Guilty', but rather of the Scottish Law which has a third possible verdict of 'Not Proven'; and a very great deal of psychic matter should be referred to this latter class, to await further evidence before it is accepted. At the same time, he ought not to allow himself to be discouraged by difficulty of proof, but bend his whole energies and ingenuity to devising fresh tests and experiments whereby his elusive subject matter may be nailed to the board of proof.

He must remember, however, that there are in occultism two kinds of evidence and proof, which I will distinguish as objective proof and subjective proof. The laws of objective proof we know well enough: they concern the findings of the physical senses, counterchecked by logic and experiment; but we must not forget that there is also the 'evidence of things not seen,' or subjective proof, which depends upon intuition. Now intuition, like instinct, is a portmanteau-word of many meanings, but the thing it represents is an actual thing, and, in some degree or other, within the experience of most people. The Oxford Dictionary defines it as 'Immediate apprehension by the mind without reasoning; immediate insight'; and, so far as I know, orthodox psychology has not dealt with it otherwise than by trying to disprove its existence; but in this, as in a good many other points in which psychology has tried issue with popular belief, the latter has justified itself, and in our new knowledge of the nature of the subconscious mind we find the clue to intuition.

I propose to define intuition as *Subconscious Mentation*, wherein the logical processes are carried on below the threshold of consciousness, and take cognizance of data which may never have been present to consciousness. In this form of thinking it is only the finished process of which we become aware, the stages by which we arrive at it being hidden. Therefore it is that intuition is referred to as being 'immediate' and 'without reasoning.'

When, in addition to our knowledge of the nature of subconsciousness, we realize the existence of subtler senses than those five with which we are familiar, we must realize that the subconscious mind may have data to work upon of which the conscious mind knows nothing, and that its findings are not to be ignored; but, on the other hand, remembering that the subconscious mind has also dissociated complexes, we realize that its findings are not to be accepted blindly.

Let us, therefore, in occult research, accept the two kinds of data: the one derived from observation, and the other from intuition. Let us admit that the latter, when properly counterchecked, can be just as reliable as the former, which, of course, also requires counterchecking, as is admitted by all but the very naïve; but do not let us make the mistake of confusing one kind of evidence with the other. It is a common thing in occult circles to hear people talk as if subjective evidence were entirely on a par with objective evidence—to make statements concerning Atlantis, or past incarnations, or the Masters, as if they were in possession of definite objective proof—and when the enquirer asks for evidence, the devotee gets angry and his interlocutor disgusted. I well remember that my entry into occult science was delayed for many years by this method of procedure. I had phenomena presented for my edification which would not stand up for five minutes under the most cursory investigation, and I, judging the bulk by the sample, condemned the whole system. I know now that I was dealing with subjective evidence, and that it is valid in its sphere, and can be proved by the appropriate methods; but when subjective evidence is submitted to the tests appropriate for objective evidence, as it always will be if offered as objective evidence, it promptly falls down, and the whole system, and the person advocating it, are discredited.

Let us now consider further the nature of subjective evidence. It depends upon three types of perception: Intuition, as previously defined, of which the results but not the process are perceptible to consciousness: Conscious Psychism, which I propose to define as perception by the subtler senses in full consciousness, not, at the present moment, going into the definition of the sub-divisions into which it can be divided: and Subconscious Psychism, wherein the perceptions of the partially developed higher sense-organs are too faint to touch consciousness and therein become part of the data of intuition.

The purely subjective data of intuition can be detected by means of psychoanalysis, and the vision of a seer can be subjected to the same process as a dream in the hands of a Freudian; that is to say, analysis by means of free association, with the technique of which the literature of psychotherapeutics is concerned, and which would be too lengthy to deal with here in detail. It must suffice to say that the subject is instructed to take each item of his dream or vision in turn, to dwell upon it, and to let his mind wander free from that starting-point, while the psycho-analyst notes where it wanders. If the subject is honest in his endeavours, it will be found that the trains of free association, derived from the different dream symbols, are converging upon the same point, which is one of emotional importance to the subject; or else are coming to a dead stop at the same point, which shows that the object of emotion is dissociated. This process enables the dream symbols to be reduced to dream material, and throws an immense amount of light on the workings of the hidden side of the mind.

In ordinary subjective dreams, the dream material is found to consist of repressed desires, memories of incidents occurring during the past day of which the emotion still reverberates, and impressions impinging

on the five physical senses during sleep. There are, however, other types
of dreams, which I will denominate as lucid dreams, and they are
stimulated by impressions impinging on the subtler senses during sleep.
The visions of the psychic are also due to the same mechanism operating
with sufficient force to penetrate into waking consciousness. If such
dreams and visions be submitted to psychoanalysis, it will be found
that they usually contain a certain subconscious element in addition
to their content dervived from superconsciousness, and it is the task
of the analyst to distinguish between the two.

It will be found that those elements which are derived from the
subjective realm of the subconscious mind will, when used as the starting-
point of a free association-chain of ideas, lead thought straight back
whence they issued, into the subconsciousness familiar to the Freudian
analyst; but the elements that are derived from superconsciousness will,
when subjected to the process of analysis by free association, lead thought
also to the place whence they issued—in this case the superconsciousness,
and will most effectually elucidate the meaning of the vision. They will
also bring through into consciousness an immense mass of material
which has previously been apprehended superconsciously, but has not
succeeded in passing the gulf that separates the higher self from
brain-consciousness.

We find that, just as the dream-symbolism could be reduced to dream-
material by this process of analysis by free association, so the vision-
symbolism can be reduced to vision-material by the same means; but
in the one case the trail of free association leads into the subconscious,
and in the other into the superconsciousness. A further test, however,
may appropriately be applied to the superconscious material thus
rendered available. If words indicative of the principal symbols in the
vision and ideas in the vision-material be used in a word-reaction test
with a stop-watch, according to the method of Jung, and the reaction
words submitted to a further analysis by free association, the resulting
proof will not only be beyond cavil, but will open up still further the
riches of the higher mind.

The use of the foregoing method will yield most interesting results,
for although it will clearly demonstrate the subconscious element which
is present in all psychism to a greater or lesser degree, it will also open
up communications with the contents of superconsciousness and bring
them through into brain-consciousness. The use of free association for
this purpose is a most important aspect of esoteric work, but its technique
is too complicated to be discussed in detail in the present pages.

A serious responsibility rests upon all who undertake the publication of the results obtained in occult experiments. They should make sure beyond all possibility of doubt that they have recorded and interpreted their visions correctly, both in concept and in detail, and should avoid in any way demanding of their readers a faith which renders ridiculous both those who ask and those who give, lest they bring into disrepute the Sacred Science which is for the healing of the nations.

5.

Meditation and Psychism

Many people think that it is impossible to conduct any research into the Unseen unless definite clairvoyant powers have been developed. This, however, is not the case; after we have reached a certain stage of training we can penetrate far into the Unseen by means of meditation. Occult meditation is a combination of the two methods of free association and directed reverie; it begins with free association, starting with an idea which is known to have been derived from the Inner Planes by the operation of the Higher Consciousness (that is why such books as the *Voice of Silence* are so valuable for meditation), and passes over, or should pass over, into directed reverie; the secret of success lies in keeping the mind steadily on its plane and subject; an operation which requires considerable experience and skill.

This method has yielded us an enormous amount of our occult knowledge, for by its use, not only the experiences, but also the teachings received on the Inner Planes are brought through into brain-consciousness; but, like all other research, it requires counterchecking, and much confusion and discredit have resulted from the failure to observe this very necessary precaution. The findings of meditation must perforce remain nothing but speculations until they have been counterchecked and proved, and what we need in occult science is a method of proof which shall test the results without spoiling the experiment.

The psychoanalytical tests cannot satisfactorily be applied to the results of meditation because these are admittedly the fruits of the subconscious mind, although the occultist takes a much broader view of the subconscious mind than the psychologist does. The analysis of meditation simply reveals that the conscious mind is obtaining access to the subconscious and availing itself of the hoarded material of the Hidden Self. This, of course, neither proves nor disproves the value and accuracy of the results. If the subconsciousness contains the truth, the findings of the meditation will be true; and it in no way reduces the value of subliminal material to prove that it has been stored in the subconscious memory, for it may very well have got into that memory as the result of a true psychic vision which has not been brought through to consciousness. In dealing with the fruits of meditation or reverie, we need to check the facts, not the origin of them, for the value of the teaching thus obtained does not depend upon its source but on its intrinsic nature. We need to escape from the dominion of authority if we are to do any serious work in occult research; the value of a message from the Inner Planes or Inner Self does not depend on the name claimed by the communicating entity, but on the nature of its message; the 'spirit' of Victor Hugo has had some ghastly doggerel fathered upon it, and many another great intellect has discoursed in vapid platitudes when recalled from the Unseen. Because a spirit calls itself Victor Hugo does not mean that it is Victor Hugo, and even if it were, what is the use of listening to it if it talks nonsense? And if, out of our own subconscious mind we can elaborate material that is of value, shall we have the spiritual snobbishness to scorn it because of its homely origin?

The subconscious mind is infinitely richer than the conscious mind, containing as it does everything we have ever forgotten, everything which has ever impinged on a sense organ, whether consciousness has noticed it or not, and also, according to occult science, the experiences of the astral body during sleep and the memories of past incarnations. It is therefore clear that if we gain access to our subconscious mind we have obtained possession of a rich storehouse of memory. But as, by definition the subconscious mind is below the level of consciousness, it follows that consciousness cannot penetrate to the level of subconsciousness, but must find some device to induce the subconscious content to become conscious. This is achieved by means of the directed reverie of occult meditation.

It is this brooding of meditation which causes the development of much occult knowledge, and which might more truly be called the Hall of Learning than the astral temple of the imagination which usually goes by that name. It is much more likely that the occult doctrines have been elaborated by these natural means than by anything spectacular in the way of Manus and Messiahs materializing on the physical plane; that which is spiritual works upon the Plane of Spirit, and has to be brought through to the mental plane by mental means and to the physical plane by physical means, each plane being governed by its own laws. There are, it is true, souls among us of more than human stature, but the difference is in degree of development, not in kind; we are all potential adepts, some are adepts in the making, and just a few are adepts in actuality. Nature does not leap gaps.

I do not mean by these words to discedit the idea of great Teachers in the past, nor the possibility of great Teachers in the present or the future, but I do most earnestly desire to discredit the idea of miracle and substitute that of law, natural and knowable, and of a piece with that which is known and proven of man and the universe.

Let us, then, if we desire to be true students of occult science, attach less weight to our visions and more to our meditations, until we come to the point when the consciousness which opens momentarily in vision has become part of our normal equipment and we are so used to it as to be able to assess its value and use it at will. But, on the other hand, let us never forget that there is no such thing as revelation to brain-consciousness; the revelation is always to the Higher Self, and has then to be translated through into brain-consciousness; in that translation discrepancies may occur, and therefore all revelation and inspiration, even the clearest, requires counterchecking.

Our problem, then, is to devise a scheme of counterchecking that shall effectually test the truth of the fruits of meditation or inspiration, while leaving room for new discoveries of occult science.

Do not let us accept the limiting position that the occult teachings have once and for all been delivered to man, for surely as evolution advances, there must come a time when brain-consciousness is able to receive more than heretofore and so will be given more; but let us also remember that what it receives will be but an extension of that which it has already received, and will most assuredly fit in with it and not contradict it; neither, if the experience of the immemorial past is any guide, will there be any new factors or sudden departures introduced. Nature is never arbitrary, whether on the visible or invisible planes; 'As above, so below,' has ever been the maxim of the occultist; and is a clue which will take us safely through the labyrinth, and to it we must cling.

Again, applying the maxim, 'As above, so below,' we shall find that a thing which is true on any plane of the cosmos is true through the whole of its system of correspondences. For instance, the same laws that apply to the solar system also apply to the atom; if then, we are testing any item of clairvoyant research, let us apply its findings to the solar system and the human system, and if we find that it is true of both of these, then we may reasonably conclude that it is true concerning the thing to which it claims to apply.

Take, for example, the researches of the late Dr Steiner regarding Atlantis and Lemuria; modern exploration and deep-sea soundings confirm the existence of a Lost Continent, and the New Psychology shows, in its descriptions of the levels of the mind, states of consciousness which exactly correspond with the states of intellectual development which Dr Steiner assigns to the different Root Races, thus confirming his statements just as embryology confirms the theory of evolution by showing in the individual the stages of development by which the species is believed to have evolved. We may, therefore, feel ourselves upon reasonably safe ground in accepting Dr Steiner's account of the Root Races. And when, in addition to this geographical and psychological confirmation, we also find a substantially similar doctrine set forth by Mme Blavatsky as derived from the Ancient Wisdom of the East, for which derivation she gives chapter and verse from the Sacred Books, we feel that we have the double confirmation of an ancient esoteric system and modern research, and we may therefore accept the doctrine of the Root Races as a fact established according to the laws of evidence with which we have to be content in dealing with the subjective planes.

Some of the occult theories that are being advanced nowadays, however, cannot be so tested; they have no correspondence with any occult system, they fit in nowhere among proven truths; some of their supporters claim that their uniqueness proves the wonderful psychic powers of their promulgators, but the experienced occultist replies that it is their uniqueness which is their undoing, for it proves them to be no part of the cosmic scheme, which ever moves in cycles. That which has been comes round again on a higher arc, and nothing opens up in evolution whose germs are not implicit in involution.

It is high time that we should turn round and ask for the evidence in support of the statements that are made in the name of the Unseen, and let us dare, in the sacred cause of Truth, to say 'not proven,' when that evidence is not forthcoming. There is no religion higher than the truth, not even personal loyalty to a beloved leader.

We must recognize, however, that in occultism a kind of evidence has to be admitted which would not be admitted in orthodox science, which is one of the causes of the latter's sterility when it applies itself to the study of life and mind. Subjective, as well as objective evidence has to be accepted, because so much of the work of occultism lies in the subjective sphere, that is to say, in the realm of inner experience. A man may say, for instance, that he has had a certain inner experience, and as that experience is peculiar to him alone, no independent witness can be adduced in support of his statements; his word is the only evidence, and therefore we are told that we ought either to accept or reject his word. The world of orthodox science says, 'Reject the unverifiable statement, the unrepeatable experiment'; the world of occult science is very apt to say, 'Accept the statement without trying to verify it, for it is on such statements that our structure of thought is built, and if you throw down one, the whole edifice of our faith will collapse.'

What answer can we make to this? Is there no Via Media? I suggest that we have two quite definite and quite independent criteria of criticism, firstly, in the ancient occult systems that are guarded by the schools of initiation; and, secondly, in psychology; not, of course, in psychology as popularly understood, but in the deeper application of it which is being developed along esoteric lines.

The ancient occult systems always have a pantheon of gods and goddesses who are all definitely related to each other as parents and offspring, brothers and sisters; there they are, in great ramifying families, and wonderful stories are told of their adventures, stories wild as the fairy tales that delighted our youth; and after we have listened to all these fantastic and sometimes obscene absurdities, we are told, 'As above, so below,' and find that if we follow out the symbolism, we have an Ariadne thread which will take us through the labyrinth, not only of the universe, but also of our own natures. We shall find, moreover, that these different ancient pantheons have a strong resemblance to each other, and likewise that the cosmologies to be adduced from them are practically identical, and we may fairly reckon that in those things wherein they confirm each other all the world over they are substantially correct.

Against these ancient, definite schemes of things let us measure the findings of our modern psychics, and if we find that they fit in and are confirmed, then we may reasonably believe that we have received a genuine contribution to our occult knowledge; but if violence has to be done to the ancient systems, if they have to be pulled and pushed to make them fit, we would do well to look for the discrepancies in the findings of the modern psychic rather than in the immemorial faith of the ancients.

By these tests can we countercheck all contributions to esoteric cosmology—they must fit in with the ancient systems and modern demonstrable science. But, on the other hand, we must not demand of psychism proofs which by its very nature it is unable to give. We must bear in mind the fact which modern thought tends to forget, that there are two kinds of logic, deductive as well as inductive. Modern inductive science is a reaction from the deductive methods of the ancients, but the inductive method is not possible in any department of knowledge until we have a mass of particulars from which to build up a general concept. When we are dealing with matters already known in their broad outlines, we can, without unnecessary delay in starting, accumulate a mass of observations and set to work with the inductive method, but when we are dealing with the totally unknown, as we often are in occult research, the deductive method is the only one we can use at the start, for we have no means of knowing whither to direct our observations nor what facts are relevant. Occult science makes great use of intuition and deduction, but having built up a system of concepts by such means, these concepts, if valid, should be capable of confirmation by the use of the experimental, inductive method of orthodox science. Our previous intuitive, deductive researches serve to indicate to us the direction in which to look for our data and the line along which our researches are likely to proceed, but while such indications are invaluable and save an immense amount of time, we should not be content with purely subjective, intuitional methods, but follow up our psychic researches with experimental confirmation, and not reckon any psychic vision or teaching as proven until this has been done.

Faith and authority have no more part in occult science than they have in natural science; those teachings of occult science which are not capable of immediate proof should be classed as hypotheses, and the chela should no more be asked to give blind belief than the student of chemistry. It is quite true that the higher branches of both sciences are only accessible to those who have fitted themselves by training for their comprehension, but from the very start modern chemistry training combines theory with practice, and so it should be with occultism.

Does this mean, however, that occultism itself is a delusion? I think we have ample evidence that this is not the case. Out of the flood of credulity and wasted effort there stand up certain mountain peaks. There is more in heaven and earth than is dreamed of in the orthodox philosophies, and it is this that occultism takes for its field, and the fact that its most ancient teachings have received confirmation from modern scientific research shows that its work has not been wholly fruitless.

When, however, I listen to the talk of some of those who are interested in occultism, I feel as if I had returned to the Dark Ages, so much of it is sheer credulity and superstition. Such romantic previous incarnations, such wonderful auras, such authoritative teachings received from the Masters; everything accepted without any counterchecking or attempt at verification.

Now, I do not dispute that such things are possible; in fact, I may say that from my own personal experience, I am satisfied that there is adequate evidence in support of all these things, and can and do accept them as part of my personal faith; but I cannot help saying that a great many of the anecdotes that I have heard recounted impress me as very far-fetched.

In the old days, it was the custom to deny anything that was not as tangible as the dome of St Paul's; nowadays, it seems to be the fashion to accept anything that is mysterious. People quote the statement of a psychic about their past incarnations or the state of their auras as proof positive. If it were not that there is so strong a feeling in occult circles for humanitarianism, I have no doubt that we should find people scrabbling in the interiors of cocks in search of omens. There are statements current in occult circles concerning mysterious occult colleges and their marvellous museums and libraries, and the Masters and their mundane habitations which, in their widespread acceptance and lack of tangible evidence, bear a strong family likeness to the rumours concerning the passage of the Russian troops through England which were current during the early days of the War; everybody had heard them, and nearly everybody believed them, for to do otherwise was to be accused of pro-Germanism; and although they no doubt served some useful purpose in keeping up our hearts during the dark days of the Retreat, it is a curious chapter in crowd psychology that the man who preferred to base his patriotism on fact rather than fancy should have met with persecution and have been dubbed an enemy. A nervous crowd is a dangerous thing, and it is a bold man who will lay sacrilegious hands on the popular idols which quiet its fears; but it will not be until we break free from authority in occultism, whether that authority be claimed for the seen or the Unseen, that we shall do any more serious work in this department of thought than the schoolmen of the Dark Ages did in natural science.

The need of certainty is very strong in human nature; it is only a highly trained mind that is able to suspend judgment on insufficient evidence; but it is better to endure the torture of uncertainty than to believe a lie, and I am convinced that if popular occultism would be content to do as a great industrial undertaking has done—cut its capital in half—it would find it was able to pay dividends on the remainder and become once more a solvent concern.

Great is Truth, and shall prevail, and no one who is sincere need fear her

6.

The Use and Abuse of Astrology

Let me say by way of preface that I write neither as an astrologer nor as a sceptic, but as an occultist who recognizes astrology as necessary to the practice of occultism. A deep knowledge of astrology can only be the fruit of lifelong study and experience, but everyone who aspires to the practice of the occult arts needs to know the principles of astrological science, although, if he be unable to give time to the detailed study that it requires for its proper mastery, he may be wise to consult an astrologer for guidance rather than trust to a half-knowledge which is no less misleading in astrology than in other technical matters.

Whether we are conscious of it or not, we are all the time reacting to the zodiacal and planetary influences which are playing upon the earth; and our reaction being determined by the relative proportions of the different elements in our psychic constitution, we need to know not only the general influences affecting mundane conditions, but how we ourselves are likely to be affected by them. For this purpose both a natal and progressed horoscope are necessary, but these horoscopes must be drawn up, not by the average professional astrologer, but by one who approaches the subject from its esoteric aspect and gives the information which is needed by a follower of the Path, instead of the usual advice concerning mundane affairs, useful as this may be if accurate.

If we consider, as Solomon bade us, the way of a ship in the sea, we shall obtain enlightenment concerning the problem of astrological influence upon our lives. In the most primitive type of sailing vessel a mat was hoisted on a pole to enable it to take advantage of the force of the wind. A craft so rigged could only drive before the wind; it could not avail itself of a side wind or tack against a head wind. So it is with the unenlightened man, he is at the mercy of the cosmic forces playing about him. The enlightened man, however, is like a boat in which the sails can be trimmed and made to co-operate with the rudder. Between the two, such a craft can avail itself of any breeze in order to make progress towards its destination, and the qualities of a sailing ship are judged in large measure by the closeness with which she can lie to the wind. A clumsy boat has to have the wind pretty nearly astern before she can make much speed, but a well-designed boat will tack almost into the eye of an opposing wind.

So it is with the enlightened man; he will make use of the opposing forces of the stars in order to advance his evolution, and by his skilful sailing turn an opposing influence into a co-operating one. If he knows that there is a strong destructive influence abroad at a certain time he will not, if he can help it, start any constructive work. If, on the other hand, he has before him the task of exposing and clearing up evil, he will choose that particular season for his operations. Thus he will have the cosmic influences with him, instead of against him.

The occultist needs to know the set of the cosmic tides in order that he may lay his course accordingly, and it is in this that the astrologer can help him. He does not, however, abandon himself to the drift of the tides, but takes them into his calculation and allows for their influence.

The planetary forces do not operate in the sphere of external circumstances alone, but affect our lives by stimulating or neutralizing the different traits in our natures. If we consider our lives in the light of our horoscopes we shall see how much of our fate was brought about by our own actions and reactions. Our rashness may have precipitated quarrels attributable to the influence of Mars; our emotions may have stirred up certain happenings of the sphere of Venus. We ourselves were the instruments of the stars.

From these observations we derive much illumination in our dealings with the planets. It may not be in our power to command external influences, but it is well within the power of the trained will and disciplined nature, guided by knowledge, to neutralize the greater part, if not all of their effects. The Macrocosm of the universe is ordered by God, but of the microcosm of his own nature man should aim to make himself the deity. 'Ye shall be as gods,' said the Serpent, and he spoke the truth; initiation develops the God within so that he may rule the microcosm of our nature instead of leaving it the prey of 'chaos and old night'—the subconscious past of the race.

The natal horoscope can be used to read the karma which a soul has to work out in its present incarnation, and we can see by studying it that certain problems are going to be set a soul, and that certain favourable influences will aid it on its way. We know, if we are occultists, that these conditions have their roots in past actions. We therefore regard the natal horoscope as the result of forces set going in the past, and we approach the astrological problems of a life from the standpoint of karma, as forces to be neutralized by reaction and realization. We do not, therefore, regard malefic planets as enemies, but as agents of karma, and we try to win from them enlightenment, realization, and discipline. The part played by Saturn in initiations is not sufficiently understood.

The initiate is not blindly driven by his karma, he consciously co-operates with it for its working out. He knows that the planetary influences will cause his nature to react in a particular way, and he throws his trained and disciplined will, reinforced if possible by magical ceremonies, into the scale, and thereby counterbalances the cosmic forces operating within his own microcosm. We cannot influence the macroscosmic influences, but discipline and knowledge can profoundly modify the microcosmic reactions of our own inner world. We can so discipline the martial element in ourselves that it will not react to the stimulation of the planet Mars and lead us into quarrels and disputes. A soft answer turneth away the wrath even of a planetary spirit. On the other hand, a disciplined fighting quality, thus brought under the control of the will, is available at the bidding of the will, even when there is no stimulus forthcoming from the planet of its affinity, and it can then be used to counteract the influence of a planet of inertia, such as Saturn. Thus does the adept balance the cosmic forces one against the other and use his trained will to turn the scale.

He also knows how to reinforce his will by linking up with the corresponding cosmic forces, and a large section of ritual magic is devoted to this process. It is for this purpose that the construction of talismans is undertaken. A talisman is a focussing point for force of a particular type, and all the processes of its manufacture are designed to that end. This is why it is so much better to make your own talismans than to have them made for you. The effect of a talisman is not upon external fate, but upon the internal reactions of consciousness. We do not affect fate by our magical operations, we affect ourselves; we reinforce those aspects of our nature which are in sympathy with the powers we invoke.

Both astrology and the art of making talismans were the guarded secrets of the Mysteries; they were a part of a Sacred Science which was never permitted to be abused by the profane. But knowledge, especially such as can be used for gain, is as hard to confine as a subtle gas, and these branches of the occult art have been debased to the uses of fortune-telling and superstition. Occultism itself has no more to do with superstition than has medicine with the use of toads to cure warts. Superstition is the tribute paid by ignorance to knowledge of which it recognizes the value but does not understand the significance.

No one deplores more than the occultist the soul-destroying abuse of the occult arts. There is nothing so destructive of a sound judgment, or so paralysing to self-confidence and will-power as the habit of consulting fortune-tellers of whatever kind. Neither is the uninitiated soothsayer a very reliable source of information. All divination ought to be conducted under the guidance of the divinity presiding over the particular operation undertaken. This ruling genius is contacted with appropriate invocations and the drawing of the correct sigils at the head of the paper on which the calculation is worked out. These methods are never used outside the lodges of the Greater Mysteries. Therefore it will be readily seen that the rule-of-thumb methods of uninitiated soothsayers are not likely to penetrate very deeply into the cosmic secrets.

The divination of the future by one who is in a position to make proper use of the information thus obtained is one thing, but a similar investigation by another, unequipped in any way to profit by the task, is on a different basis and productive of far more harm than good. There are people who go to psychics and astrologers as the hypochondriac goes to doctors and patent medicine vendors. It is a very unwholesome and harmful thing to do, and productive of sickness of the soul.

The power of auto-suggestion is enormous, and unless we have the training and knowledge necessary to enable us to use astrological information as a chart that enables us to avoid rocks, it is far better for our peace of mind to be without that information.

The initiate, who is the only person who really has the right to this knowledge, knows that by its means he can neutralize or deflect the forces thus revealed to him; the untrained man is very apt to think that he is the helpless victim of fate. Did the revelations of astrology stimulate him to greater efforts, they would serve a useful purpose, but how often is this the case? How much oftener do we see their findings used as an excuse for *laissez-faire*?

I have no love for miscellaneous divinations by irresponsible people; I think they do much more harm than good. They are on a par with the reading of medical literature by the laity. A divination should be undertaken solely in relation to spiritual development, after prayer and purification. It should be done under the instruction of the initiator responsible for the training of the pupil, who should explain to his pupil the spiritual and karmic signification of his chart and show him the methods and meditations that counterbalance adverse planetary influences and the disciplines which shall enable him to turn his fate into his initiation.

7.

Records of Past Lives

To many, the doctrine of reincarnation is one of the most illuminating contributions that esoteric science makes to human thought. It is logically satisfying, inspires to noble living, and gives hope and courage in adversity. Not only does it explain much in human life that is otherwise incomprehensible and purposeless, but it also enables the broad outlines of the future to be foretold with a considerable degree of accuracy. It is not, of course, as detailed as a progressed horoscope, but if the line of development pursued by the soul in the past be known, it is often possible to draw conclusions as to possible developments in the future, especially in matters connected with initiation and occult work.

But just as any medicine which is strong enough to cure is also strong enough to poison if wrongly used, so the doctrine of reincarnation is no more fool-proof than any other aspect of occult science; indeed, it is more liable to abuse than most, for it is a very simple matter, granted sufficient imagination, to construct elaborate romances concerning past lives; experience of occult circles shows that this form of psychism is among their most popular, if not most profitable activities.

Whoever is sincerely concerned for the prestige and purity of occult science cannot but regret that so valuable a doctrine should thus be brought into ridicule and discredit by the folly of its adherents. We badly need some standard of proof which shall be applicable to all such statements. For the most part they are a matter of *ipse dixit* on the part of some psychic, and no proof is offered or required because it is not realized that proof is available.

A brief statement of the methods of obtaining past records may serve to show how proof may be obtained and tests applied. Unless some counterchecking evidence is available, it is unwise to give credence to such reports, however much they may appeal to the subconscious self, whose other name may be vanity.

The record of every action performed, or feeling felt, or thought conceived is preserved as an image in the reflecting ether, which is really the memory of the planetary spirit. It is as if a mirror retained impressions like a photographic plate. These images, however, are not stored in any haphazard fashion, but obey the same law of association of ideas as do our own subconscious memories; those things which occur in sequence are linked together, so that if one thing is recovered by consciousness, all those connected with it tend to be drawn into consciousness also. Details of this psychological process are given in my book *Machinery of the Mind* (V. M. Firth), and need not be entered upon here. But not only do those incidents which occur in sequence become linked together, but also those which occur simultaneously, or at the same place, or which deal with the same subject. It will thus be seen that if a single image from a particular organization of ideas can be brought into consciousness, it is a comparatively simple matter to recover the rest of the ideas connected with it by inhibiting other thoughts and allowing them to rise spontaneously into consciousness, as they will if not deflected.

Memories of past lives, then, can be recovered from the reflecting ether, or subconscious mind of the planet, provided we can get any single idea which shall serve us as a starting-point. It is this absence of a clue which presents the difficulty, just as we can often repeat a poem which we have once learnt, but apparently forgotten, provided the first line be given us.

So although all records are readily available in the reflecting ether for such as can read therein, it is the exceeding richness of the material which baffles our researches; we might seek for days and weeks, and while recovering much that was of interest, fail to locate that which we sought unless we had some definite starting-point.

Many things can serve as a starting-point. Sometimes fragments of memory are retained in childhood and can be recalled later. Sometimes they come through in dreams or are awakened by the sight of a place, or even the reading of a book that deals with the period in question. Moreover, in the deepest subconscious memory of each of us, all our personal records are stored. That subconsciousness, however, is closely barred from the direct access of the personality, and we have to rely on indirect methods of approach; any effort of will or attention usually defeats its own ends by leading us into the land of phantasy.

When we are seeking to remember our own lives, we have to depend on the chance hints which circumstance may bring us; we can no more force the memory than we can force the recollection of a forgotten name. By the very fact that it is in the subconscious mind, it is by definition beyond the reach of consciousness, and we have got to wait for it to be brought within reach by some extraneous agency before we can avail ourselves of it.

Should any fragment of the past come within the range of our apprehension, however, it is only a matter of the patient application of the technique of free association for the whole of that life to be reconstructed from the subconscious memory in an infinitude of detail only limited by our patience.

When a psychic seeks to read the past records of another, a different method is used. He has to find some point in his own record where the trails cross, otherwise he will be unable to pick up the end of the thread of connected memory images. A very tenuous clue will serve his purpose. Some common memory, however unimportant—a mutual association with the Egyptian temples or French mediaeval life of approximately the same period—some minor fact that is within the range of both memories, and the contact is through; the end of the thread is in the psychic's hand, and the skein of memories can be unwound. Sometimes the psychic will read from place-memories, and sometimes straight off the querent's subconsciousness; both methods are equally efficacious. It also sometimes happens that a spirit communiciating through a trance medium will give records of the past lives of a querent, using the same methods to read them as are employed by an investigator incarnated in a physical body.

We have, then, all these different methods of obtaining access to the records; and anyone who has had experience of the matter will readily see that the problem is not so much to read the records as to prevent the images and phantasies in the subconscious mind of both querent and psychic from intruding upon the screen. Suppressed or thwarted desires are a potent and prolific source of such intrusion, as the psycho-analysts have demonstrated; but a long-forgotten novel dealing with the same subject is just as likely to contribute its quota when that particular memory-stratum is struck with which it is associated. We may have identified ourselves with the hero or heroine of some story read in the impressionable days of adolescence, and later, when we begin to investigate our karmic records, reproduce the whole plot as a phantasy of a past life.

The problem which confronts us in the reading of the records is, frankly, one of elimination and rejection of the spurious and irrelevant out of the mass of subconscious material presented to us. The psychic has to follow a very tenuous thread through very tortuous ramifications, and it is exceedingly easy to go off on a wrong scent after following the right one for some time.

For this reason, records of past lives are usually obtained in a very fragmentary state. When the querent is reading his own memories, or a psychic is reading them for him, there will usually be a few clear-cut and detailed scenes, and but little coherence until the free association method painstakingly works out the details. When a communicator from the Inner Planes gives the records, however, they will usually be synoptic, that is to say, a series of brief records such as are given in a popular encyclopaedia. These records are an invaluable basis for future work, as they furnish most valuable clues, and can always be filled in subsequently by the free association method. Those who are fortunate enough to get such a series given them should be at great pains to preserve even the most irrevelant details for this reason. It is not often, however, that communicating spirits can give these records, for unless they are themselves of a certain degree of development, they will not be able to rise to the plane beyond which the Second Death has no power. That is to say, so long as consciousness is still focussed in the non-material aspects of the personality, the entity will have no memory or knowledge of those things which pertain to the individuality—the reincarnating ego— and therefore, for him, the personality of his last life is his only being. It is not until consciousness rises to the level of the higher self that past lives are remembered. Therefore it is that the average communicating spirit has no more knowledge of past lives than the average incarnated spirit, or common man. It is only when we are working under the aegis of a school of initiation that we begin to touch the spirits that have this higher consciousness, in heaven as on earth, and then they will tell us of past ages and read the Records for us if permission can be obtained; but for such a reading permission always has to be obtained from the Master who has the pupil in keeping, for this knowledge is not lightly to be communicated, and if given indiscreetly may do more harm than good.

The best and simplest way to countercheck records of past incarnations is to get several different psychics to read the Records without allowing them to know what has already been read. A remarkable degree of confirmation is usually obtained. Those things in which they spontaneously confirm each other may be taken as established by the testimony of independent witnesses, and those in which they contradict each other may be taken as inaccurately observed. It will always happen, however, that different psychics will report things which remain unconfirmed. These need not necessarily be discarded, they must merely be regarded as not proven until confirmation is forthcoming. One psychic may see one thing and another psychic may very well miss it and see another when there is such a wealth of detail to be seen.

Our next method of counterchecking is to seek to explain the known facts of the present life in the light of the past. We ought to be able to see a clear line of causation leading up to them if the Records have been correctly read for a series of incarnations. Moreover, if we are able to see the hand of the remote past showing itself in the immediate past, we ought also be able to see it showing itself in the future, and this is the most satisfying test of the accurate reading of past incarnations, and its most valuable justification. Let us give an example to make this matter clear. Supposing A, B and C have been associated together repeatedly in past lives, if A and B have already met, it is probable that C is not far off, and will in due course appear upon the scene and play his old part. If this should occur, there is proof positive and ample justification for accepting the reading of the Records as substantially accurate, though no such reading will ever be complete owing to the enormous complexity of the matter involved. Therefore we must always be prepared for unsuspected factors to introduce unexpected causes.

If these two methods, the counterchecking of psychics by one another, and the re-checking of the results by observation of the life be employed, we shall obtain evidence which ought to be good enough for anyone save the professional sceptic.

In the absence of the possibility of such systematic counterchecking there are certain things which render a record suspect. If we see the cloven hooves of the natural instincts peeping out, we shall know that we need to look little further than the subconscious mind for the source of the records.

These instincts show themselves in two ways. The self-preservation instinct has for one of its aspects the very human impulse of self-aggrandizement. If a person of very ordinary attainments in this life claims to have been someone of very extraordinary attainments in the past, we may well ask one of two things—whether the record is true, or, if true, what he has been doing in the meantime thus to have come down in the world of spiritual development? To claim greatness in the past does not so much cast a reflected glory on a mediocre present life as suspicion on the intervening lives which have apparently written Ichabod on the wall. The great bulk of mankind at the present time consists of very ordinary people leading rather drab lives; it is curious that so many records of past incarnations represent very extraordinary people leading very lurid lives. One may not unreasonably ask why it is that the average should have undergone such a drastic change? The highly coloured should be as suspect in stories from the past as it usually is in stories about the present.

Equally, when the cloven hoof of romance, especially illicit romance, shows itself, we would do well to proceed with caution and ask many questions. Why is it that the fact of a twin soul linked to us by bonds of karma, was never suspected until that soul is actually met face to face in incarnation, whereupon memory leapt to consciousness spontaneously? If we had actually had such a twin soul, the memory of it would have in all probability shown itself in childhood and we should have been awaiting its coming for years. Moreover, why is it that twin souls never by any possible chance marry each other, but always appear as someone else's legal spouse? The fact of having really met one's twin soul might or might not be sufficient reason to abandon one's responsibilities and honour, but it is very odd that twin souls are so seldom able to ratify the bond in the eyes of society.

We must face the fact that in our present imperfect state of society a great many marriages leave one or other of the contracting parties spiritually unmated, and that the unsatisfied one will be greatly tempted to re-mate elsewhere. Emotional starvation begets emotional tension, and when in such an overwrought and unsatisfied state of mind an attractive stranger is met, whose weaknesses proximity has not revealed and whose magnetism familiarity has not dulled, the unexpectedly violent emotional reaction is accounted for by the hypothesis of a karmic tie which has come down through the ages, wherein life after life the two who are mutually attracted have been linked together, and the unfortunate superfluous spouse of this incarnation, who is cast for the part of villain of the piece, has nothing to do but stand aside while the twin souls rush together in obedience to the inevitable laws of their fate; no one is held to be to blame for this save the superfluous spouse, who has unfortunately and in ignorance appropriated that which was not his (or hers). The suffering of the unwanted one is regrettable, but inevitable because the laws of karma decree it.

How often has one heard this specious argument advanced in extenuation of what is, after all, adultery. The fact that adultery takes place with unedifying frequency between people who have never heard of karmic ties but are merely prompted by their instincts, is not apparently held to throw any light on the matter. The allegation of a karmic tie is held to be sufficient reason for demanding a separate classification.

It is not an easy thing to adjudge the rights and wrongs of a matrimonial problem, and no man can say what the temptations and bitternesses of another may have been; but at least we can say this, that there is nothing in the law of karma, or the forces working through from the past, which justifies, although it may explain, infidelity. To be tempted is one thing, to yield is another.

The memory of past lives is mercifully hidden from the average man, and experience shows that it is well that it is so, for a soul needs to have reached a certain degree of enlightenment before it is able to make the right use of the knowledge. Because a thing has happened in the past is no reason why it should be allowed to recur again. Forewarned should mean forearmed. What is the use of knowing the past if we use our knowledge as a justification for repeating our mistakes instead of profiting by them? We are merely piling up fresh karma for the future.

When karmic problems confront us our best course is to put aside all personal considerations, and, regardless of self, work them out in accordance with cosmic law. We shall then be karma-free in that respect; and although the present life may have to be dedicated to the task of unwinding the tangle, the path of the future will lie open before us.

8.

Numerology and Prophecy

There are so many different systems of numerology that to give a definition which would include all of them is not an easy matter. They range from the simple substitution of numbers for the letters of the English alphabet, and the translation by their aid into a numerical value of the name which our parents, influenced by considerations of family interest and recently read fiction, saw fit to give us—to the most elaborate mathematical calculations based on detailed measurements of objects celestial and terrestrial, carried to six decimal places.

Between these two extremes there is every grade of elaboration and every point of view. It is not possible in these pages to give a detailed analysis of all the different systems competing for our attention, nor yet justly to assess their merits. Some of them are of a complexity that demands prolonged study and considerable mathematical aptitude for their understanding, and it is unjust and misleading to criticize a system unless adequate time has been given to its study. It is a simple enough matter to knock down Aunt Sallys of one's own setting up, and the concept of a system which the adverse critic undertakes to demolish may bear very little resemblance to that which its exponents are endeavouring to explain.

No criticism, therefore, of individual systems will be undertaken in these pages, but an attempt will be made to explain the esoteric principles upon which numerology rests, and the student may then be able to see whether any given system is likely to be sound or otherwise.

Initiates have always attached great importance to number, colour, sound, and form, holding that, according to the Hermetic maxim. 'As above, so below,' the spiritual affinities of a given object can be deduced from these things, and that with its spiritual affinity it will have a special link. They therefore utilize these objects when they wish to get into touch with and bring through into manifestation those potencies on the Inner Plane which they are held to represent. The uninitiated believe that the force invoked comes into physical manifestation through the symbolic object, but the initiated know that the material object is not employed to enable the power to come down, but to enable the mind of the magician to go up along a particular line of consciousness. His mind contacts the potency, and it is through his own nature that the power comes down, not through the so-called magical object. It must be clearly realized that the value does not lie in the material object, but in the train of thought it evokes. The power, however, may subsequently be associated with the object, thus forming a talisman. The subject of talismans is of great interest, but it is beyond the scope of the present study. The matter is merely referred to here in order to prevent confusion of thought.

Objects do not have numerical values assigned to them arbitrarily, but in accordance with some of the profoundest principles of esoteric cosmology. the different planes of existence came into manifestation during different phases of the cycle of the Logoidal Being. Their substance is organized out of atoms of different types. These atoms are really nothing but force in cyclic motion, vortices infinitely minute. Their motion, however, is not in a circular path, but an angular one, and some follow a three-sided, some a four-, five-, six-, or seven-sided orbit. Each plane of the manifested universe is characterized by prime atoms which possess an orbit of a particular type. Each plane developed a special type of force and consciousness. Each plane had as the focus of its development one of the planets; that is to say, when the evolutionary life-wave was on a particular planet, a particular plane was developing.

It will thus be seen that a plane of existence, a type of consciousness, a planet, and a particular type of atom, will be associated together. The prime, or fundamental atom will have a certain number of tangents in its orbit, and this number of tangents will determine the vibratory rhythm of its movement. All the complex forms on that particular plane will be built out of these atoms; therefore there will always be, in whatever associations they may be gathered, the fundamental number of that plane as one of the prime factors into which their vibratory rhythms can be reduced. These vibratory rhythms are the basis of all existence, and they can all be expressed in mathematical terms. Hence the significance of number in esoteric science, for these sacred numbers are the formulae of the invisible forces which are behind all things, visible and invisible.

For practical purposes, a knowledge of the numerical factors is chiefly of value for determining the inner relationships existing on the subtler planes; it has a secondary value in that cycles of recurrence can be worked out if the primary unit is known. But as cosmic units of time are of transcendent vastness, but few have been observed and worked out, and these, being planetary in their significance, they have but little bearing upon the personal destinies of human beings. The coming of the Avatars or Christs—the birth and break-up of civilizations—these things are known to the adepts—but it is exceedingly doubtful whether the affairs of nations are revealed save in so far as they are incidental to these things. To work out the day of the outbreak of a war by means of one of these cosmic cycles would be like measuring an object seen under the microscope by means of a surveyor's line.

Those profound students of the subtler aspects of existence, the Qabalists, were in the habit of reducing to numerical value all potencies with which they worked, and embodying these formulae in the name given to each potency by means of the number-letter system of the Hebrew alphabet, in which each consonant is equated with a number, the vowel-sounds necessary for vocal expression being represented by points which merely aided pronunciation and had no bearing on the numerical value of a word. The Hebrew orthography grew up primarily as a means for such notification, and was therefore a sacred language like Sanscrit, which was evolved for the same purpose.

If, therefore, we are dealing with the names which the Hebrew Qabalists gave to the potencies they described in their sacred and esoteric books, we may be sure that they are reducible to numbers and constitute formulae which, when deciphered and reduced in turn to their factors, will tell us a very great deal about the potency concerned and its Inner Plane relationships. There is, however, an exoteric Gematria as well as an esoteric. Soi-disant initiates, knowing the principle, attempted to use it as a key to Mysteries which were beyond their grade, and so we find the most elaborate experiments in interpretation of the Sacred Books of the Hebrew race—interpretations which reduce whole sentences to their numerical value and from that extract an inner meaning.

That such a proceeding is fallacious is obvious; for, in the first place, there are many different versions of the Sacred Books; in fact, no definite canon was established until the Books themselves were hundreds of years old, so that the original wording of the writers was hard to determine. Accuracy of text being unobtainable in the necessary degree, how can there be accuracy in the results of these calculations? That there is a significance in the proper names is not denied, but that there is a significance in every jot and tittle is exceedingly doubtful, and even if there were, it would be impossible to calculate it from our modern imperfect text.

Another method of numerical calculation, which is having a considerable vogue at the present time, is that based on measurements of the Great Pyramid at Gizeh. These measurements are usually computed in inches and are carried to several decimal places. There are two different schools of Pyramid numerology, one which uses what is called the Pyramid inch, and another which uses the British inch as established by Act of Parliament. When we call to mind the vast size of the Great Pyramid, the erosive action of time, which must have defaced all surfaces, even the internal ones, by some millimetres at least, and the fact that the outer casing of the Pyramid has been removed so that its actual thickness cannot be determined—it will be admitted that any fine degree of accuracy in the measurements can hardly be achieved. When, therefore, the calculations based on these measurements are reckoned in inches and carried to several decimal places, any accuracy of result is obviously out of the question. If the premises of the Great Pyramid enthusiasts are admitted, the logic of their deduction is inescapable; but as the very measurements on which they base all their calculations are mere approximations, and as there are several different opinions among archaeologists as to what those measurements should be; and as, moreover, there are at least two different schools of Pyramid numerology, each of which is equally logical in its calculations, but uses a different inch—it is fairly obvious that we are not dealing with something that is wrought in the living rock, but which is cut out of cardboard at the pleasure of its makers.

It is an admitted fact that all temples of the Mysteries were symbolic structures. If we want to understand their symbolism we must enter into the minds of their makers, men like ourselves, concerned with esoteric science. We can best do this by observing the methods of anyone who is getting together the paraphernalia of ritual magic at the present day. Every possible object which has a symbolic relationship to the force to be invoked is assembled in the temple; the robes of the magi and the hangings of the room are of the symbolic colour; the number of lights on the altar, the number of knocks employed in the invocations, the number of circumambulations, are in accordance with the numerical potency of the force to be invoked.

A temple used for ritual purposes, moreover, is invariably constructed so as to symbolize the macrocosm, and incidentally the microcosm of the soul itself, in order that the special rituals performed therein may be related to the whole.

If we study the structures used for religious purposes by the different traditions, we shall see this principle prevailing. The Christian church is invariably cruciform in reference to the Great Sacrifice of its Founder. The sun temples, such as Stonehenge, are circular, referring to the Zodiac. The worshippers of the creative force in nature use either the tower or the serpent-mount; the worshippers of the Great Mother use the cave or crypt—all symbols well known in analytical psychology. The Sphinx is a symbol of the four elements; it is also androgynous. There is every reason to believe that the pyramidal form was used in the same spirit and for the same purpose—as a symbol enshrining great cosmic truths to be used in the raising of consciousness, and that it represents, not a book of prophecy, but a symbol of the universe, and, incidentally, of the constitution of man and the way of evolution and initiation.

Esoteric science was not persecuted in Ancient Egypt. The priests had perfect security for their records. Why should they be at such pains to conceal their prophecies?

That the pyramids of Egypt and the stones of Avebury enshrine profound truths there is no reason to doubt, but esotericists consider that these truths refer to the constitution of the universe and the soul of man, and have nothing whatever to do with prophecy.

The Book of Revelation is another favourite subject of speculation. This book, as is obvious from its nature, was written by a Christian Qabalist versed in the esoteric doctrines of the day, probably a high initiate of the Mysteries. Its key is found in the Holy Qabalah. A study of the Qabalah should be the basis of any attempt to understand the prophetic books of our Scriptures.

The Beast, whose number is 666, has been variously identified with Nero, Napoleon, President Kruger, and the Kaiser, or whoever happens to be the national bogey-man of the moment. Napoleon, however, is a national hero to the French. It depends upon which side of the Channel one lives as to whether he appears as the Beast or as the Angel standing in the sun. Queen Elizabeth must have appeared very much of a Beast to the Spaniards of her day.

Which of these identifications is correct? All of them, says the esotericist. Wherever a man acts as the instrument of destruction, he is functioning with the force of the Beast, whether he be breaking up the home or the nation. The destructive forces, which are just as much a part of the cosmos as are the constructive ones, have found a channel through him and are using him for their purposes.

But we must not forget that destruction is always the first phase of construction. A cosmic truth is distinguished by its universal applicability.

The sacred teachings delivered by God to man, whether they be expressed in words or stone, do not concern persons, but spiritual principles. The actions of persons and the fate of nations express these principles, and to that extent may be considered as the fulfilment of prophecy, but the promises of the Sacred Writings have been fulfilled many times, and will be fulfilled again whenever the conditions supervene which they describe.

There are two ways of penetrating the future. The only legitimate method consists in observing and studying the causes at work in the past and present, and trying therefrom to deduce their outcome. The more insight we have into underlying and remote causes, the more likely shall we be to draw true conclusions. Esoteric science is of great value in such a process because it reveals more of underlying and remote causes than appears upon the surface. Thereby it often produces the effect of pre-vision by supernatural means, yet in actuality its methods are entirely natural and logical, it merely has certain additional data available for its consideration.

The illegitimate method of penetrating the future consists in trying to put the clock forward and see events as if they had already happened. The seer using this method is seeking for effects where he should be looking for causes.

Events shape and take form on the Inner Planes long before they appear as actual happenings on the plane of manifestation in matter. A seer who can function on these subtler planes can see them brewing there and report what he sees as prophecy. There is one thing which is forgotten, however—that up to the very moment of occurrence fresh forces may come to bear, fresh factors be introduced into the case on the Inner Planes, with the result that the final issue is largely modified. A very strong force will come down the planes with but little deflection, and consequently manifest in matter in its original form, so that any seer who could discern its development as a thought-form would be able to prophesy accurately the nature of its manifestation on the physical plane. There are, however, but few occasions on which the force is sufficient to resist deflection in its passage down the planes. In the great majority of cases, as soon as it comes within the sphere of the group-mind of the race it is profoundly modified. Moreover, a determined mental resistance will be able to produce varying degrees of deflection. It is this fact of which mental workers avail themselves in the many different systems that exploit the powers of the mind. Prayer and invocation are also potent alternatives. The prophet may announce what will happen if nothing occurs to prevent it, but out of such a multiplicity of factors, anything may occur to modify the course of events.

The effect of prophecy is to paralyse effort. In the face of adversity the human soul ought to rise up in its strength and wrestle with the dark angel of affliction till it yields the secret of its name, that is to say, of its hidden nature, so that it may be subdued to his service. If this be done, good is brought out of evil, the good of ennobled character, if nothing else. But if we accept supinely an impending fate we have surrendered our manhood. If we must go under, let it be in the last ditch. If we must surrender our lives, let us sell them dearly, not give them away. The power of the will, backed by courage and tenacity, is tremendous. Victory has many a time been snatched out of the very jaws of defeat by a courage that would not accept the inevitable.

We can learn many things concerning the soundness of a doctrine by observing its effect during epochs when it was widely believed. The heyday of soothsayers has always coincided with the darkness and degeneracy of national life, whereas the great epochs of national achievement have ever been characterized by confidence in the power of human enterprise. 'He can, who thinks he can,' is a profound maxim of occult science.

We ought to approach the occult arts in the same spirit in which we approach any other phenomena. They are not supernatural, they break no natural laws; they are merely comparatively rare and little understood. As soon as we understand their rationale they cease to be supernatural and become natural. An advancing psychology is going to clear up all the mysterious elements in occultism. Those of us who take up these ancient studies should pursue them as scientists, not as mystery-mongers and exploiters of human credulity. When we approach the subject of prophecy in this spirit, it soon transpires that there is no such thing as exact predetermination. There is only tendency.

9.

Group Karma in Occult Societies

A high initiate of the Western Tradition once said to me, 'Two things are necessary for safety in occult work, right motives, and right associates,' and anyone who has had experience of practical occultism knows how true this is. Some writers declare that good intentions are sufficient for safety in occult studies, but experience proves this to be far from the case. The man who, relying on nothing but the strength of his aspirations, invokes the Highest, is safe; but the man who, having read something of magic and alchemy, starts to experiment, is not safe. A little knowledge is a more dangerous thing in occultism than anywhere else. The solitary worker, depending on aspiration and meditation, and unguided save by his intuition, although his progress may be slower, is in a much better position than the blind follower of a blind leader.

Students of esoteric science have always tended to band themselves together into caravans for the purpose of taking the Golden Journey to the Samarkand of their dreams, but before they leave by the Desert Gate they would do well to know something of the character of the master of the caravan and their fellow-travellers, and they can no more afford to ignore the character of these latter than they can afford to ignore their guide.

The psychology of the group-mind is only just beginning to be understood by orthodox science, but it forms the basis of much occult work and has been used in the Mysteries from time immemorial. Ritual depends upon two things for its validity, the proper contacting of the Unseen Powers, and the formation of a group-mind on the physical planes; that is why the Master Jesus declared that, 'If *two or three* be gathered together in My Name, there am I in the midst of them,' and why the Church will not permit the Eucharist to be celebrated unless 'two or three' be present.

A group-mind is not the same thing as a group-soul. A group-soul is the undifferentiated mindstuff out of which individualities are specialized; It is primitive, and belongs to the past; but a group-mind is a thing that can only be built up after individual minds have been developed. One might almost define it as a super-complex, a constellation of co-ordinated ideas ensouled by an emotion which is shared by many minds and therefore transcends any individual one among them. One may conceive of the group-soul of a race as lying deep down below subconsciousness; but one may conceive of the group-mind of any organized body of people as an oversoul, a vast, brooding, artificial elemental, potent for good or evil, under whose light or shadow each individual member of the group carries on his life. The influence of a group-mind is incalculable and but little understood; it must suffice to say that whenever anyone joins any organization he comes under the influence of its group-mind, and the closer-knit and more highly emotionalized the organization, the stronger its influence over its members; therefore it behoves us to be very careful what groups we join, for there are but few souls who can maintain themselves untouched by group influence.

Let us also remember that whenever we join a group, we shoulder our share of the group karma. Whatever has gone on in the past leaves its mark behind it; if the group can point to a long and noble line of just men made perfect by its discipline, the group-mind shines by its own light and confers a benison on all who are privileged to share in its influence; but if it has back debts to pay off, such as the karma generated by a Holy Inquisition or a phase of debased phallic worship, the initiate will find that he is called upon to do his share in the payment of these debts, just as the inheritor of an encumbered estate has to consent to his income going to pay off the mortgagees.

The student must always remember that, until he has advanced further in knowledge than those with whom he is associated, he cannot hope to escape the influence of the group-mind they have formed. It will do one of two things; either, insensibly to himself, it will tune him to its viewpoint and vibrations, or it will more or less forcibly eject him, and the preliminary processes that lead to such an ejection for occult incompatibility of temperament are unpleasant for all concerned; therefore it is much better to keep away from the wrong group than go in and come out a sadder, even if a wiser man.

You may think that you can go into a society and receive its good and ignore its evil, but, believe me, you cannot; its tone will influence you unknown to yourself; a change, so subtle that you are insensible to it, will be going on in your consciousness; that to which you at first took exception will become a matter of indifference to you; the power to discriminate between the finer shades of right and wrong will be blunted, and you will find yourself floating with the current, although you had determined never to get in out of your depth. Remember that it is always better to be alone than in bad company, and that you need never fear that your occult progress will be retarded by a sacrifice made on the altar of principle.

Advanced occultists know the meaning of what is called the tainted sphere, and it was the custom in the past to close down and disband any order that allowed its sphere to become tainted, and to raze its temples to the ground and sow the site thereof with salt, so seriously did the old initiates take the question of an astral taint. The brethren would disband, going to far countries to escape the pursuing influence of a debased group-mind, and would do no occult work nor pursue any occult study till the period of purification had been worked out.

The principle of fallowing is not sufficiently used in occult work. It is the only possible thing to do when matters have gone wrong on the Inner Planes. An exorcism will dispose of entities but it will not reconstruct the soul they have obsessed; and the soul in such a parlous condition will attract to itself seven devils worse than the first every time it ventures into occult work until the process of its purification be completed.

An esoteric society that has any scandal in its midst ought to take every precaution to prevent its sphere becoming tainted by the influences thus brought into it; although it may give compassion to the delinquents, it should require them to withdraw from association with any of the brethren until their purification is accomplished, and in open lodge should condemn the error, though sending thoughts of compassion and brotherhood to the brethren who are expiating it. If this be not done, if the scandal be hushed up or condoned, it will assuredly taint the sphere. The only thing that will clear it is the group-reaction of horror and repulsion, not to the sinners, but to the sin. The sinner is never to be condemned, but helped to rise again to the stature of manhood in Christ; but there must be no sentimental condonation of the sin, and the calling of a spade by its proper name has a very salutary effect on those who seek to idealize the irregular.

One thing is quite certain, if the same type of trouble keeps on breaking out in any society, especially if these scandals involve different people each time, it means that the sphere has become tainted, and if that is the case, there is only one thing to do. Close down, scatter the brethren, and let the ground lie fallow for anything from a year to seven years according to the seriousness of the trouble, and when reconstruction takes place, let it be in a new temple, with new robes, symbols, jewels, or whatever may be the material accessories, acting just as if plague had ravaged the society, as indeed it has upon the Inner Planes.

The member of an order or fraternity is not infrequently called upon to combat spiritual evil in high places, and I would give him one word of advice when so called: never attempt to fight the magician with magic unless you are of a higher degree than he is. Put up the sword and invoke the Christ. Turn upon evil the scorching flame of Pentecost—the tongues of fire of the Holy Spirit—but to the sinner, always come as a physician and overcome his wrong-doing by healing him of the weakness that tempts him to sin.

In fighting black occultism of any sort, and such combats are by no manner of means uncommon, always, like the aviator, try to get the upper air of your antagonist; if he fights with the weapons of the human mind, meet him with the Power of the Divine Spirit; never let the fight degenerate into an unseemly scuffle on his chosen plane. Transmute a force into its opposite by means of a realization of the true nature of force as derived from God. See the true spiritual man behind the mask of the personality, and never lose sight of it even in the fiercest moments of the struggle with the evil that the personality manifests.

'Be still and know that I am God,' is the attitude of power. It is a refusal to react that is the strongest armour. Unfailing compassion and unfaltering fidelity to the right will win any battle in the long run. Let us learn, in all times of difficulty and distress, to trust the Masters, to invoke the Divine Law, and to await its working.

I remember well an experience I had in the early days of my occult work. An ethical problem presented itself in the group I was training, and I had to decide whether it was better to allow the transgressor to remain in the group in the hope of a possible redemption, or to say, 'There are certain things which are incompatible with occult work, and if you do these, you must go.' It was a difficult problem; I was very reluctant to take a step which might result in pushing a soul out into the darkness, and equally reluctant to risk having the sphere of my group tainted. In my perplexity I laid the problem before the Masters. The 'still small voice' came through to the inner consciousness and said, 'Invoke the Sacred Name of Jesus, and let that which cannot abide, depart.' This I did, with extraordinary results. The person concerned seemed unable to endure the sound of the Name, it appeared to produce an unendurable exasperation, and the problem was speedily solved by a voluntary withdrawal. The mantric effect of the use of the Sacred Name of Jesus is such that anything impure seems unable to withstand its vibrations and has to take refuge in flight.

This Name is the supreme Word of Power of the West when used with knowledge. Whenever any moral evil has to be dealt with in a group, the Power of the Name of Jesus is a universal solvent. When confronted by such a problem, do not attack it with rebuke, but constantly keep before the eyes of the transgressor the ideal of the Divine Life lived in Galilee and say, 'Look at this, and see how such an action compares with it.' One of two things will happen, either the delinquent will be humbled and regenerated, or cast forth as if by an explosion by the persistent sounding of the vibrations of that Name.

Let it be remembered, however, that it is only possible to use that Name of Power if we ourselves are attuned to the Christ-consciousness; if there is that in us which is incompatible, we too shall react to it. We can only let loose that force upon a soul when we ourselves have risen above any personal reaction to wrong-doing, when we honestly 'desire not the death of the sinner, but rather that he shall turn from his unrighteousness and live.' But there are times when for the sake of others an evil condition has to be put out of a group, and though it is no man's province to pass judgment on his brother, he may have to act as the instrument of justice. The decision and sentence, however, should always be left in higher hands. Let those, therefore, who are confronted by that problem follow the advice that was given me, and 'Invoke the Sacred Name of Jesus, and let that which cannot abide, depart.' No injury can be done to any innocent person by such a method of dealing with the problem; if he have the sparks of regeneration in himself, they will be blown into flame. The Name of Jesus is inimical to nothing but impurity and evil. Invoke that Name upon a man or a movement, and let It divide the bones from the sinews, for It is sharp as a two-edged sword.

10.

Authority and Obedience in Occultism

The rival principles of autocracy and democracy have fought a long battle for control in human affairs, and democracy has so far made good its case that to call a man an autocrat is to reproach him. With many occult teachers, however, the old principle of autocracy still seems to maintain its prestige, and they require of their pupils an unquestioning obedience and a blind faith.

The problem is admittedly a difficult one in occult matters, for the man who knows more must inevitably act as guide to the man who knows less, and many things cannot be explained to those without the gate. There are two sides to be considered in this, as in every other question, the side of the teacher, bound himself by obligations, and responsible for the safeguarding of the system with which he is entrusted, a system which may have come down to him from the remote past, and which he, by the terms of his obligation, is not allowed to alter. He, with his superior knowledge, knows the pitfalls of the Path but may not be permitted to point them out expressly, for many of these pitfalls are of the nature of deliberate tests; he, with his clairvoyant vision, which a teacher must possess if he is to be other than a blind leader of the blind, knowing the inner states of his pupils and their karmic record, may have to keep silence concerning much which he discerns, even as had Jesus, who said, 'I have many things to tell you, but ye cannot bear them now'; and yet he may desire to give a warning, which, if accepted, might save much difficulty and delay. For all these reasons the teacher desires authority over his pupil, and yet he must not forget that no human soul can accept responsibility for another, neither can he tread one step of the path for his pupil, nor save him from one experience that he needs for his evolution. When a teacher is newly entrusted with his office he may urgently desire to save his pupils from suffering, but when he has seen deeper into the nature of things, he looks upon suffering with another eye, for he knows its educative value. He learns more and more, as time goes on, to interfere as little as possible between the pupil and the Master of that pupil upon the Inner Planes; for he knows that his function is to enable the pupil to come into conscious touch with the Master who has committed that pupil to his care for training, and that however great a teacher's wisdom may be, it is better that the pupil should learn to think for himself, even if he makes mistakes, than to have his thinking done for him and thereby be kept in a state of ignorance and inexperience. As well might the teacher of the violin try to play on behalf of his pupil as the teacher of any system of occult training try to take a decision on behalf of his pupil. All that either of them can do is to show his pupil, give him principles to guide him, and then bid him try his hand and, after the mistakes have been made, not before, explain to him where the errors have lain and how to amend them.

The teacher who has a genuine system to communicate and who is really in touch with his Master and acting under His instructions can safely leave his pupil to the operation of the cosmic law. If he is right in his opinion that a certain course will prove unsatisfactory, and the pupil, disregarding his advice, pursues that course, the latter will not be long in finding out his mistake and will assess his teacher's advice all the higher for this practical test of its wisdom, and be ready enough to give heed in the future. It is seldom that real loyalty is yielded till such a test has been made.

The demand for blind obedience as a proof of trust should be regarded with suspicion by the would-be pupil; the confidence trick is a very old one, and can be played on more than one plane. No one should demand faith without proof; if he has anything tangible to offer, he will be able to give satisfactory proofs and offer good and sufficient reasons that shall satisfy the judgment and bear investigation. Early in my occult career I met a teacher who demanded blind faith as a proof of loyalty, and those things concerning which we were required to exercise faith turned out to be sordid irregularities. For that which is good, a good reason can be given, and that for which no good reason can be given, generally turns out not to be good.

The seeker after initiation is in a difficult position, for he is at a disadvantage as regards knowledge, and if one who appears to know more than himself gives a definite order, he is not in a position to disprove it except by disregarding it and seeing what happens. If, however, he fixes his eyes unfalteringly on the ideal of the Master, he will have a standard whereby to judge the teacher to whom circumstances have assigned him.

I may be reminded that some books on initiation declare that unquestioning obedience should be given to the teacher as being the mouthpiece of the Master. It is quite true that *if* the teacher is indeed working, as he claims to be, under mandate from the Master, his advice will be invaluable on account of its wisdom, but how is the pupil to know this to be the case? The assertion of the teacher is valueless in the matter, he can say *anything*, and the more of a charlatan he is, the more magniloquent will be his statements and assertions. Those who have really known the Masters are awed into silence.

No human being should ever be asked to give blind obedience, and to demand it of a chela is to 'sin against the Light' that is within, the 'Light which lighteth every man that cometh into the world.' No human being, liable to the changes that illness and old age inevitably bring about, has any right to demand a promise of obedience; and experience has abundantly shown that such a demand invariably leads to trouble.

The pupil can only judge his teacher by results. Does he bring forth the fruits of the Spirit? Is his life Christ-like? Then his influence can only be good. But is he erratic and disconnected in his thoughts? Uncontrolled in his temper? Sordid in his outlook? Untidy and dirty in his person and environment? Surrounded by people of undesirable character who appear to enjoy his esteem and confidence? Such a man is a good one to avoid. Let us never take leave of our common sense in occultism and remember that a tree is known by its fruits, and if the fruits are disorder and demoralization, we will not shelter ourselves under that tree unless we are prepared to partake of those fruits in due season.

But if a pupil has found a teacher who appears to have much to give him that he wants, is he then to yield a blind obedience as the price of his training? Again I should say 'no.' Human nature is a mixed and contradictory affair; none of us is perfect in either our character or our wisdom, and the occult teacher is no exception to the rule. Experience of the reliability and knowledge of a teacher may engender confidence and cause great weight to be attached to his advice, but a pupil should no more trust his teacher completely than he should condemn him completely for a single error. Let all advice be considered on its merits and accepted or rejected accordingly. This is the lesser of two evils, for although it is an evil to have come to a decision on incomplete knowledge, it is a lesser evil than the abrogation of free judgment. Moreover, the pupil has access on the Inner Planes to his Master, and, even if he is not able to bring the memory of the reply through to brain-consciousness, it will have entered the subconscious mind and speedily work its way to the surface in the shape of an intuition. But even so, the pupil should not allow his reason to be thrust aside, for it is quite within the power of a trained occultist to plant a suggestion in the mind of his pupil which shall have all the appearence of an intuition. In order to guard against this, it is a good plan to perform the meditation in which the Master is invoked in a church where the Blessed Sacrament is reserved.

The pupil, seeking earnestly after the truth as best he may, should remember that the demand for obedience is a very sinister sign, and if that demand be backed by an oath in any shape or form, especially an oath that has no term to it, such as a proviso for release from obedience if the pupil withdraws from the training-school, a wise man will no more take that oath than he will give a blank cheque; and if, in addition, any attempt is made, by threats or otherwise, to make withdrawal from the school difficult, he will be wise to smash his way out of the trap without further ado, and appeal to his Master for protection. The workings of mental domination are so insidious and deadly that no action is too drastic to escape from them; but let it be remembered that in the Name of the Master Jesus and in the Sign of the Cross is sure protection, and that great power can be drawn from the reception of the Holy Eucharist. It is not likely that a really black occultist will maintain himself for long in English-speaking countries at any rate (concerning others I cannot speak), for there are definite organizations for dealing with such conditions, and these, meeting him with his own weapons on the Inner Plane, and an exposé and press campaign on the outer plane, speedily run him out of the country into another jurisdiction. Once across the Channel or Atlantic he is out of harm's way, for the lower kinds of magnetism will not carry across water.

Pitch-black occultism, however, is really easier to deal with than the Isabella-coloured variety in which the teacher as well as the taught is struggling in the darkness, and owing to lack of principle and scruple has got himself on to wrong lines. Demands for money are, it goes without saying, enough to condemn any occultist off-hand and without further enquiry, for it is too well known to need reiterating that no price may be asked for occult teaching by any one under the jurisdiction of the Great White Lodge; but there is another and subtler kind of claim that may be made upon the pupil, a claim for support in furthering political aims. A recently published book pilloried the occult fraternities for this offence, and in the case of some organizations the attack was justified and salutary.

Here, again, a big question is opened up. It may be argued that the occultist with his deeper insight is the natural leader of reform and should bear his part in social movements. I reply, let him be active in humantiarian effort by all means, but let him flee any interference in politics as he would the devil, for the experience of centuries has shown that it leads to nothing but trouble. A teacher, whether religious or occult, is concerned with prinicples, and principles only, and should leave the application of those principles in political affairs to others. He may well preach universal brotherhood, but he should have a care how he sets to work on the immigration laws. He may advocate a reformed medical system, but he should not concern himself with legislation intended to bring it about; the reason for this may be simply stated in the words of St Paul, 'The weapons of our warfare are not carnal, but mighty, to the pulling down of strongholds,' and when he receives these weapons, he must, like Peter, put up his sword.

Political activities are a terrible temptation to the occultist; knowing what he does, it is very difficult for him to avoid the use of his knowledge and power to remedy abuses, and by so doing he is very apt to run ahead of the times and do more harm than good. It seems as if fanaticism is inseparable from the application of the principles of the higher life to politics, and spiritual zeal has shed quite as much blood as worldly ambition.

An occultist must make his choice between being a teacher of spiritual things and a leader in the affairs of the world, for he cannot be both; he cannot be within and without the veil at the same time; if he attempts it, though no doubt he will, with his knowledge, exercise great influence on the affairs of the world, he will find that he has paid the price in the clouding of his spiritual vision and the loss of the power to discern between the 'still small voice' of the Spirit and the promptings of ambition. A man cannot split himself into pieces, all arguments concerning Dr Jekyll and Mr Hyde to the contrary; and indeed, if that parable be rightly understood, the very essence of it lies in the fact that Dr Jekyll could not get away from Mr Hyde, but was gradually mastered by him. So with the occultist, the ruling passion will gradually absorb the whole man, and he will either weary of his political efforts and realize their needlessness for one who has the powers of the Spirit, or, having had his love of power whetted, he will drag his unhappy pupils at the chariot-wheels of his ambition into whatever coils he may involve himself in. Those who are opening up the higher consciousness are in a very sensitive state while this process is going on, and they simply cannot stand a fracas, and collapse with nervous breakdowns. Where active political work is going on in any esoteric society it is perfectly certain that no active occult work is going on, for the two are incompatible. I will therefore dare to give a word of plain advice to the aspirant, even at the cost of likewise giving offence in certain quarters. Clear out of the order that touches politics; steer clear of the teacher who takes up politics, for you may be quite sure that you will be *used*, and not trained.

Never lay aside your common sense or your moral integrity. Let no one persuade you to do evil or even associate with evil in order that good may come of it and you may obtain knowledge. Never believe that any initiator of the Right-hand Path will require it of you. In that quaint old book, *Brother of the Third Degree*, which, in spite of its stilted phraseology, contains much knowledge, the candidate is pictured as being required to commit a murder as part of his initiation ceremony, and on his indignant refusal to do so, is received with acclamation. The test of the Dark Initiator is one that the student is sometimes called upon to face, but if he constantly reminds himself that 'men do not gather grapes from thorns or figs from thistles,' if he constantly looks upon the Master Jesus as the ideal Initiator, and judges all demands made upon him by the standard of the Life that was lived among the men of Judea, he will not go far wrong, and he will find his way safely through all the turns of the labyrinth of the temple.

It is obedience to divine principles that should be emphasized, not obedience to personalities, or even systems. When all is said and done, it is the Higher Self that really initiates us, and although teacher and Master combine to bring that Higher Self into function, the process begins and ends with Realization. Personal loyalty has no place on the Path, and any true teacher will realize this, being selfless. He will say to his students, 'It does not matter who feeds the sheep so long as they are fed,' and will remember that the Master set a little child in the midst of the disciples when they disputed who should be the greatest.

It may be that the younger souls among the followers of a teacher may not be equally wise, but the seeker who has hold on spiritual ideals knows that they may safely be ignored and that the forces they have set in motion will return upon the circle in due course and teach them those things which it is necessary they should know.

It has been argued that the professor who undertook to teach a pupil chemistry would require obedience lest the pupil should blow himself up; but my experience of chemical studies has been otherwise. The professor may warn his pupil that if he makes an injudicious mixture of the chemicals that surround him, he may have a bill for test-tubes, window-panes, and even hospital expenses, but I have yet to meet the school of chemistry which bound its students by oath not to experiment. The only institution which, so far as my reading goes, ever made the attempt, was the Holy Inquisition, and the day for that sort of thing is over, if indeed it ever had its day, which I beg leave to doubt.

The Eastern Schools are just as rigorous regarding the freedom of the chela as are the Western Schools. The point crops up again and again in *The Mahatma Letters*, and a Master expressly stated to Mme Blavatsky, 'We do not make slaves.' Personal authority in occultism is neither necessary nor justifiable. The Masters can very well take care of Themselves and the cosmic laws will discipline the recalcitrant pupil whether they be administered by human judgment or not.

After all, it is the pupil himself who will suffer if he makes a mistake, and it has been truly said that the man who never makes a mistake will never make anything. Let the teacher look upon himself as a guide and an adviser, not a master; let him learn the distinction between a warden and a warder, and have a very tender reverence for the souls that have entrusted themselves to his guidance, and remember that in the Mysteries there is a special curse laid upon the man who 'Breaks a superficies,' meaning thereby, one who, by the power of his will, profanes the sanctuary of another's consciousness. The integrity of the soul must be maintained at all costs, and none should yield himself to the dominion of another, even if that other claim to be his initiator. Let the seeker, whatever be his ignorance and weakness, dare to stand up before any tribunal in earth or heaven and declare that with God's help he will judge for himself. Freedom of thought and speech has been too hardly won for us to abrogate any jot or tittle of that priceless boon. The remedy of an arbitrary authority is worse than the disease of ignorance.

Let the seeker turn to the Master in all things and he can be independent of teachers and schools of occult training. The teacher is only a means to an end, and the true teacher knows it. He knows that the sooner the pupil passes out of his hands into those of the Master, the better he has done his work.

Let the seeker, when required to take an oath of obedience, reply that he will swear to obey his own conscience; that he will meditate upon the life and actions of the Master Jesus and judge all things by that standard, for it is the standard of the West; and that he will pray to God for guidance, and fearlessly follow the Light so far as he receives it; and that if such an oath be not good enough for that esoteric school, then that esoteric school is not good enough for him.

11.

Secrecy in Occult Fraternities

The very word 'occult' means *hidden*, and occult science has always lived up to its name. Rumour, no doubt, has had free rein, but experience has worn the cowl. Even in times and countries where the facts of occultism have been accepted and the Mysteries respected, the cowl has not been thrown back, and the adept has secluded himself from veneration as sedulously as from persecution.

The reason for this secrecy is frequently, and not unreasonably, questioned. Do not other scientists give their discoveries to the world for the benefit of humanity? Why, then, should occult scientists conceal knowledge, which is admittedly of inestimable value for human upliftment when it is being so earnestly sought after? To keep in private hands knowledge which should be broadcast for the benefit of humanity is to stand confessed as a charlatan who would make profit out of the infirmities of his brethren or retain power in his own hands for self-aggrandizement.

If must be conceded that this charge could be made good against certain of the Mystery-schools at certain periods of their history, but in that we are not concerned; our task is to investigate the charge that is brought at the present day by the seekers after initiation, and see whether their claim can be made good, or if the reserve of the *illuminati* may be justified.

An institution, like an individual, can never hope wholly to escape from the influence of its past. The experiences and vicissitudes it has undergone have made it what it is, and it takes time for other experiences to undo the work. The true occult Orders date back to time immemorial, when they carried on their work and developed their systems under conditions very different to those that prevail at the present day. Firstly, they had to carry on their work in the midst of a populace much less highly evolved than that by which they are surrounded at present, in an age when persecution meant something much more tangible than hard words. Some knowledge of occultism, or at least a sincere belief in its powers, was current among those outside the temple, and nothing would have pleased the rulers better than to make the secret fraternities a weapon of political power. Time and again they succeeded in their aim, and each time it meant the corruption and downfall of the mysteries so prostituted. It is little to be wondered that the oft-learnt expression of misunderstanding, persecution, and exploitation at last sank in, and the occult fraternities became, as they have remained to this day, cryptic orders in both senses of the word.

Times, however, have changed, and the guardians of the Ancient Wisdom may not unreasonably be asked to reconsider their position and say how much, if any, of the knowledge in their trust may be safely rendered available for the generality of mankind.

The amount of teaching which is given must always be determined by the capacity of the recipient, and the occult fraternities can never give out to the world more than the world can take; and as the pace of the convoy is always that of the slowest ship, it follows that the amount of knowledge released from the Mysteries must be determined by the capacity of the least evolved among its possible hearers.

Fifty years ago the experiment was tried of giving out the *theory* of occultism to the general public, and Helena Petrovna Blavatsky was the messenger employed for this purpose. She taught the basic principles of occult cosmogony and philosophy, and these ideas have worked like leaven through the thought of the age and profoundly modified its standpoint. The bitter accusations she levels at the science and theology of her day would not be applicable to ours, so well has her mission fulfilled its purpose.

She did not, however, teach the *modus operandi* of such simple miracles as she performed, and it is the custom of the Theosophical Society at the present day to procure its teacups through the ordinary channels. That section of the knowledge of the Magi which is popularly called Magic was, as always, withheld.

Most students of occult science have no doubt realized that it is concerned with the mind side of things—the mind of man, the mind of nature, and the unorganized, raw material of mind; and they know that, theoretically, it is possible to manipulate all this by means of the powers of the human mind alone. Many schools teach their students that there is no other means of advancement than through the trained human mind. Some students, however, have realized that to try to control the mind side of things by the unaided mind is like trying to carry on any form of labour with the bare hands. Man is a tool-using animal, and the occultist is no exception to the rule, and it is the knowledge of the occult tools which is so sedulously guarded by the *illuminati*. Just as the operative mason uses tackle and mechanical devices to enable him to handle weights beyond the power of his unaided sinews, so does the occultist, in his rituals and 'words of power', use the psychic equivalent of the lever, counterpoise, and pulley.

The formulae of occultism exactly resemble the formulae of mathematics, in that they are expeditious ways of achieving certain known ends that have been explored in the past and are too well known to need to be rediscovered by each successive student; though, if the teacher be wise, he will satisfy himself that his pupil is capable of doing the necessary calculations and thoroughly understands the principle involved before he furnishes him with the mantram or 'word of power' that is a mechanical device on the inner planes. When a true occult order confers the secrets of its degrees it is really giving its initiates an ephemeris and table of logarithms corresponding to the plane with which the degree is concerned. Mme Blavatsky, when she published the *Secret Doctrine and Isis Unveiled*, gave to the world just as much knowledge of the Secret Wisdom as a student might obtain from a book of astrology if he had access to neither ephemeris nor logarithms. It is quite true that he might observe the heavens, and work out his own tables, and compute his own calculations of the movements of the heavenly bodies, but he would need to be a mathematical genius to do so, and it would be a weary waste of time, for the knowledge is already in the world.

So with occultism. The principles are available in the literature of many an esoteric society. Enough is given out to enable the student to see the implications of the concepts of occult science, but by no manner of means is enough given out to enable him to *do* anything beyond the exercise of a little mild and unreliable psychism, heavily adulterated with the workings of the imagination, which he possesses no means of counterchecking.

We may take it, then, that the principles of occultism have been given out to the world under mandate from the Elder Brethren by such writers as Helena Blavatsky, Rudolf Steiner, Eliphas Levi, Papus, Westcott, Mathers, and others of similar standing and scholarship, who have the right to rank as initiates of the Secret Wisdom; but that the *modus operandi* is still sedulously guarded, and not every initiator who invokes the Name of God is called of our Father.

The knowledge that confers the practical powers of occultism must remain, as ever, under lock and key; and this safeguarding of the knowledge which is power is not peculiar to the occult fraternities, for the medical profession does the same, and even the fiercest opponent of trade unionism would hardly care to maintain that anyone who has a mind to do so should be at liberty to buy poison by the pound at the nearest grocer's.

The knowledge guarded by the secret fraternities is too potent to be given out indiscriminately, and is guarded, not as a sordid trade secret, but as the power to dispense drugs is guarded—for the safety of the public. It may be asked, of course, that, if occultism is so dangerous, had it not better be left alone? To which we reply that if a drug be sufficiently potent to act as a remedial agent, it will be sufficiently potent to upset the balance of metabolism or destroy the substance of tissues if given upon the wrong occasion or in the wrong quantity. And so with occult science. Because it is potent enough to raise the mind to higher consciousness, it is also potent enough, under wrong conditions, to destroy the mind. When we realize, for instance, the immense possibilities of hypnotism, even as practised by the medical profession, and realize that this is but a leakage from the Mysteries wherein a three-day cataleptic trance was part of the ritual of initiation, we can guess at the possibilities of occult knowledge in wrong hands. The power conferred by this knowledge is neither good nor bad in itself any more than a lever is good or bad in itself, and it can be a servant of either regeneration or destruction. It depends entirely upon the motive with which it is handled. Can you, then, blame the guardians of this dangerous brightness if they use every precaution to ensure that it shall only find its way into clean and trustworthy hands? Be assured that the secrecy of the occult schools will never be relaxed till human nature is regenerated.

The guardians of the Secret Wisdom are only too anxious to communicate it to those who are worthy to receive it, but suitable pupils are not very easily found. There are, on the other hand, earnest seekers after illumination who complain that the Teachers do not make themselves sufficiently known, and therefore opportunity for advancement is denied. To these it may be replied that the finding of the Teacher is one of the tests of the aspirant. There are plenty of indications offered by the propaganda organizations, and if the aspirant studies these carefully and draws his own conclusions he will find the way. One hint may be given, however. The way lies inwards, and not outwards. We find the Master on the inner planes before we are assigned to a Teacher on the outer plane; and if we aspire with a resolute determination that never counts the cost, and, on the material plane, leave no stone unturned, importuning all those who have anything to give, ruthlessly discarding that which is found to be worthless, we shall work our way to our goal by the only path that leads there, learning as we go.

It is useless to complain of the lack of signposts; the signposts are there for those who can read.

It must not be forgotten, however, that although the persecution of the occultist in the present day does not take the form of the halter and faggot, it can make itself felt in subtler ways, and therefore occult fraternities have very strict obligations concerning secrecy as to their membership and places of meeting. If a man cares to announce himself as a student of the Secret Science he has a right to do so, but he also has not only a right, but for certain work, a necessity, for secrecy. Antagonistic thought directed towards an occult operation may prevent its achievement, and therefore the situation of the temple and the names of the brethren must always be kept secret.

There is one true charge, however, which can be laid at the door of the Guardians of the Secret Wisdom. Have they made sufficient provision for the preaching in the market-place, for the training in the Outer Court of the Temple? Why was it that the Eastern Tradition had to be brought to Europe? The soul that has once been initiated into an occult tradition finds its way back to its old school readily enough when it has reached spiritual maturity in each incarnation. To such the secrecy of the fraternities presents no barrier. It has the entrée, and passes within the veil without obstruction; but the case is far otherwise for the soul that, having learnt all that evolution can teach it, is desirous of setting foot on the Path for the first time. Such a one wastes much time and effort from lack of the necessary knowledge, and may well say to the Guardians of the Mysteries, 'Let your light so shine before men that they may see your good works and glorify your Father which is in Heaven.' The Eastern Tradition has its outpost in the Theosophical Society. Has the Western Tradition an equivalent?

Do not let it be forgotten that traditions are racial. What that great initiate, Rudolf Steiner, did for the German-speaking races someone must do for those who use a Latin root-language or the Anglo-Saxon tongue. It may be argued that Mme Blavatsky did this; but to advance such an argument is to show ignorance of the fundamentals of occultism. I would be the last to belittle the work of that great pioneer and brave servant of the Masters, but the fact remains that she brought no more than the kindling for the fire of the West, and until the coals of our native occultism catch, the fire cannot be said to be alight.

Many times in the history of the Western races has the light of occult science been stamped out on the physical plane, and as often has it been rekindled by a spark from an Eastern altar. Whether from that of the Druses of Lebanon or the Mahatmas of the Himalayas is immaterial, for there is but One Light in the Highest, and fire is of the same nature everywhere, be it of coals or of the spirit. What are our Western adepts doing to feed the sheep of their Master now that a hunger for the bread of wisdom has been awakened?

12.

The Left-Hand Path

Those who interest themselves in occult science constantly meet with warnings concerning the avoidance of the Left-hand Path; they read of Black Occultism and Dark Initiators and many other items calculated to make the flesh creep. A wholesome respect for the Powers of Darkness and a disinclination to trifle with them is a sound basis from which to start the investigation of supernormal phenomena, but panic-stricken ignorance does more harm than good. The warnings to neophytes are usually as vague as they are portentous, and afford little practical assistance when the student is actually confronted with an abuse of occult knowledge.

The subject is not a very savoury one, and for its comprehension plain speaking is necessary, just as plain speaking on other social problems was necessary for their remedy. A hush-hush policy gives evil its opportunity, whereas, if the matter be understood, the back of its power is broken.

Black occultists may be divided into two classes, those who deliberately say to Evil, Be thou my good; and those who stray onto the Left-hand Path more or less unintentionally, and having got there, stay there, often deluding themselves. We will deal with the former class first because they afford a clear-cut illustration of the workings of spiritual evil. Those of the second class represent every grade of modification of the same principles. They are, of course, not so dangerous as the true devil-worshippers, but they can be very harmful and unpleasant. Fortunately, the Christs of Evil are as rare as the Christs of Good. Supreme achievement in any walk of life is attained by but few.

The Initiate of the Right-hand Path is God-centred; the Initiate of the Left-hand Path is self-centred; that is the prime difference between them.

It is the point which determines whether a soul will turn to the Right or the Left when it enters upon the Path. Further occult development is but an unfolding of one or the other aspects of the nature.

The Initiate of the Left-hand Path is aiming at power for self-gratification. He is dangerous to contact because he is out to use his pupils, not to serve them. He is utterly unscrupulous and entirely selfish, and there is not very much left of a life after he has finished with it. There are three motives which prompt him—greed, lust, and desire for power and knowledge for their own sake.

He seeks to open the psychic faculties, both in himself and others, by speedier and less troublesome means than the slow ripening of mind-training and meditation, and for the achievement of this end he employs drugs which 'unloose the girders of the mind' and give it a temporary expansion of consciousness. Now it is one thing to unloose the girders of the mind, and quite another to get the rivets tightened up again, and unless one is prepared to go through life rattling like a cheap motor-car it is unwise to seek this method of development, speedy and effectual though it is. However warmly a system of drug-taking may be re-commended as entirely harmless, the neophyte will be wise to refuse it, for it is based on a fundamentally wrong principle, and the after-results of even a single experiment may be very far-reaching.

To open the psychic centres and contact other planes does not constitute the whole of psychism. It is necessary to know how to approach and handle that which is contacted. Drugs do not confer this knowledge, which only comes with experience; and therefore, although they indubitably can open the subtler planes to the experimenter, the opening is of so undesirable a nature that it is far better avoided.

Again, the neophyte may be assured by friends in whom he has confidence that they have made the experiment without ill results. This may also be true; but there is a factor known to physiologists as drug virginity. The evil effects of any abnormal stimulant or sedative do not become apparent at once; if they did, there would be no drug addicts. One can hardly conceive of a person becoming an addict to tartar emetic. It is the cumulative effects that are toxic; and because the drugs which alter consciousness are habit-forming with various degrees of speediness, the risk even of experimentation is too great. Moreover, a dangerous astral contact may be formed at the very first experiment.

It may be taken as axiomatic that anyone who suggests the use of drugs for raising consciousness is definitely on the Left-hand Path and had best be avoided.

An adept may also offer to open the psychic centres of his pupil by means of hypnosis. To this method two objections apply. The first is that which we have already considered in relation to drug-illumination: that although it admits to the subtler planes, it does not confer the powers of the planes. It is equivalent to starting up the engine of a high-powered car and sending an inexperienced driver straight into city traffic without even showing him which is the brake and which the accelerator. Secondly, after a person has been brought well under hypnosis two or three times, he is pretty much in the hands of the operator; and even if that operator be motivated by the purest intentions, the proceeding is very disintegrating to the pupil. In medical work nowadays deep hypnosis is very little used for this reason, psychologists preferring to rely on suggestion.

It should be noted, however, that although after repeated hypnotic sleeps the hypnotist can often throw his subject into trance by a word or a look, this is not possible in the first instance. No one can be hypnotized without his knowledge; it requires co-operation, and generally a determined and patient co-operation for the first induction of hypnotic sleep. The unwilling victim has merely to put his thumb to his nose and the would-be Dark Initiator is completely floored. I saw a great deal of remedial suggestion done by qualified doctors in the days when I worked at a mental clinic, and although there was no doubt about the ascendancy that could be established over a patient when once the hypnotic sleep had been induced, to induce it was not at all a simple matter, even with the patient co-operating to the best of his ability.

I noticed, however, that the personality of the hypnotist had an extraordinary fascination for the patient, and out of that fascination many subtle and undesirable reactions proceeded. I have seen a good deal of psychoanalysis, and I hold no brief for it in its cruder forms, but there is no doubt about it that there is a very great deal in analytical psychology, and the more I see of human nature, and especially psychic human nature, the more I realize it. An accusation of hypnosis may be but an inverted way of saying, 'I love you.' When such a charge is made, it is well to enquire concerning the *modus operandi* employed. Such an enquiry will soon reveal to those who know the real thing whether there is any foundation in the charge or not; Such charges are not lightly to be accepted. 'Hell knows no fury like a woman scorned,' and the romancings of hysteria could have kept Haroun al Raschid awake indefinitely. When the story is told with highly coloured accompaniments, it is generally safe to suspect it. In real life such happenings are sordid and matter of fact in the extreme.

But although I discount the story of hypnosis by force, I am well aware that one person can obtain a very great influence over the mind of another, and have often seen it done. I am of the opinion, however, that such a domination rests on the victim's trust and confidence in the dominator, and that when these are thoroughly shattered, the domination does not last long. I am disinclined to believe the victim's assertions that he is entirely helpless in the matter, despite his realization of the nature of his thraldom. When the bond is realized but not broken, there is either a lingering fascination, or the victim has been privy to matters which would cause social ruin if they came out, and the dominator knows too much to be defied.

The best way to escape from any such domination, when once it has been established, is to seek the help of some common-sense, stable-minded friend, well endowed with worldly wisdom and experience, who will not unduly stress the psychic side of matters, but encourage the victim to pull himself together, admit his share of the responsibility, and cut his losses at any price. If he fears publicity should he turn on his tormentor, let him remember that his enemy has probably very much more reason to fear publicity than he has; if he follows the advice which the caterpillar gave to Alice in Wonderland concerning the Puppydog, and says to his tormentor, 'You let me alone, and I will let you alone,' he is unlikely to hear much more of the matter. An unwilling victim is a nuisance.

The black occultist ensnares his victim through the weaknesses in that victim's own nature. The get-rich-quick spirit prevails in many souls who seek initiation, and they desire to reap where they have not sown. It is not difficult to fathom the psychology of most of these who get onto the Left-hand Path and stop there. Those who resolutely refuse to play with fire seldom burn their fingers with black occultism. I am not saying that entirely innocent people, especially if they have but a superficial acquaintance with the subject, may not have unpleasant experiences at the hands of a black occultist, but it is my experience that the suspicions of a right-minded man or woman are quickly aroused and they beat a retreat in the early stages. When people become deeply involved in black occultism, they usually have to say 'Mea culpa' before they get clear.

This does not mean that those who realize a mistake and retrace their footsteps are not deserving of all the help we can give, but in approaching them we ought to exercise the same precautions as in saving a drowning man, and take care that we ourselves are not involved in unpleasantness, for anyone who has come under the influence of black magic, even if he desires to break away from it, has probably undergone considerable deterioration of character, and is apt to be a very uncertain friend until his wounds have had time to heal and he has got the poisons out of his system. He will be suspicious and treacherous, liable to revert to his old ways at any moment and turn suddenly on his benefactor and rend him; his mind is very likely to be more or less unbalanced, and he is liable to delusions of persecution. It is no light undertaking to rescue a soul from the clutches of a black magician. In fact, it is just like rescuing a cat from a dog: in its terror it will probably scratch and bite at the hands that have saved it from the jaws. Occult salvage is not a task for the timid, the emotional, or the imaginative. It requires a level head, calm judgment, patience, and firmness, as well as the knowledge necessary to meet the black occultist on his own ground and withstand the occult retaliation which will probably be forthcoming. But, God be praised there are those who will do it, and greater love hath no man than this, for there is every reason to fear those who can destroy the soul as well as the body.

13.

Occultism and Immorality

We now come to the consideration of another and very important aspect, the occult aspect of sex. I have dealt with this in my book, *The Esoteric Philosophy of Love and Marriage*, but I have touched but lightly on the black aspect of the subject in those pages. A brief explanation of the basic ideas is necessary for those unacquainted with this book.

Those who have entered into the deeper aspects of occultism know that Kundalini, the Serpent Force which lies curled up at the base of the spine, is really the sex force which has its centre in the sacral plexus from which issue the nerves which govern the reproductive organs. In the normal way, this force is fully absorbed in its physiological functions, but there are two ways of rendering it available for other purposes, for in its psychic aspect it is a very important potency on the Inner Planes: it can be sublimated above its natural plane of expression, as is done by the ascetic; or it can be degraded below it. The latter is the method employed by the black occultist. We must, however, distinguish between the person who is merely making occultism a cloak for his vices, and the person who, with knowledge, is deliberately using this great force as an occult battery. It is not easy to give sufficient information on this subject to forewarn the innocent without supplying the evil-minded with information they would be better without.

Let us try and understand the principles which govern the right use of this force, and then the methods of its abuse will become clear. 'Where your treasure is, there will your heart be also.' When the whole nature is concentrated upon spiritual things, it takes less interest in the things of the senses. The great driving forces of the emotional nature are then turned to spiritual objects instead of earthly ones. This is the only true sublimation. From such a concentration of the whole nature on an ideal comes tremendous psychic energy. The black occultist desires to obtain this concentration of psychic energy without foregoing the sensory gratifications. He wants, in fact, to eat his cake and have it. How is he to manage this? By the simple expedient of eating his own cake and then borrowing somebody else's. We then have the spectacle of one person, his stomach full of cake and another slice in his hand, confronting another person who has had just enough cake to whet his appetite and is very hungry. The enterprising cake-stealer then proceeds to trade in the superfluous slice of cake with other hungry cake-eaters. A variation of the metaphor may give a better understanding. The Japanese employ tame cormorants for fishing. The birds have a ring round their long necks which prevents them from swallowing the fish they catch, which are transferred from their pouches to that of the fisherman. The cormorants, needless to say, are kept hungry in order to encourage them to catch fish. The occultist who works with sex always has his cage of human ringed cormorants. The poor creatures do not wear very well, and have to be constantly replaced.

I will describe the methods of some of these fishers of souls, and I have no doubt that many of my readers will recognize familiar faces.

For the first I will describe, I have a certain amount of respect, for I think he is sincere according to his lights, though I am of the opinion that his lights are asquint. He advocates the pagan view of life and a return to the primitive, and tells unmarried ladies of uncertain age that what they need is some of his male magnetism, and proceeds to administer it in the time-honoured fashion with results that can better be imagined than described. He is probably quite right in his diagnosis that for the full flowering of their natures they need the experiences of love and marriage, but these are not to be obtained in the hole and corner fashion in which he gives them. There is a great deal more in sex than the aspect we share with the rest of the vertebrates; the magnetic rapport of marriage is on the emotional, not the physical plane. The occult aspect of sex is its sacramental aspect, not its animal aspect. This disciple of Dionysos is atavistic; he is a 'throw-back' to an earlier sub-race. His spiritual home is in the groves of Ashtoreth. His way may be the way of the servant, but it is certainly not the way of the Christ.

Another group of occultists, who have attracted some attention and deserve more, seem to be constructing a reservoir of astral force to be used for magical purposes. This reservoir appears to be supplied by inducing women to concentrate their emotions on the leader of the group by telling them that they have a link with him in their past lives. The well-known psychic who has been giving this advice even goes so far as to tell some of his victims that he can read their future and that they will eventually marry the person upon whom they are instructed to concentrate. The effect of this advice on unmarried girls is bad enough, but it is a still more serious matter when it is given to married women, especially when they are also told that if they want to advance rapidly on the Path they should not live with their husbands but allow themselves to be put in touch with an astral lover. Not only does this precious advice break up homes, but in several cases, to my personal knowledge, it has rendered the recipients mentally unbalanced. To this unsavoury council an attractive bait is usually added. The clairvoyant declares that their psychic centres are just on the verge of opening, and that a very little would render them clairvoyant. If this information is well received, he goes further, and says that they are already in touch with their Master on the Inner Planes, that they are actively engaged in occult work at night when out of the body, and that it is only because they fail to bring through the memory that they are unaware of it. This is a bait that few can resist, and they pay visit after visit to learn how their auras are getting on and what they have been doing recently on the Inner Planes.

Occult knowledge may never be sold for money, and no initiate who is under the Great White Lodge will ever charge a fee for any form of occult work. This is such a well-known esoteric fact that it is a little difficult to sympathize with those who choose to part with half-guineas for information concerning their progress on the Path, it being so obvious that the man who will ask and accept the half-guinea cannot be on the Path himself.

Another aspect of the work of this same group has been repeatedly exposed in the newspapers, notably in *Truth*, whose reputation for integrity in these matters stands high. As much of the details as could be printed in the English Press were published by that journal. Fuller reports are available in the pages of an American magazine, *The O.E. Library Critic*. Recently, the Continental police, who are not squeamish, stepped in and one of the persons concerned got six months' imprisonment, so it can be judged how serious and how widespread are these abuses.

Briefly, the charges against these men concern the practice of that form of unnatural vice known as homosexuality, the offence for which Oscar Wilde received a sentence of imprisonment. It is a very cruel form of vice, as the victims are usually boys and youths on the threshold of life. It is also very infectious, spreading in an ever-widening circle as those who have become habituated to it in their turn proselytize for victims.

The many supporters of these people defend them by asking how it can be that men of such dedicated lives, who give such lofty and beautiful teaching, can be addicted to such foul practices. For those who have made a serious study of occultism, the explanation is self-evident. It was this particular vice which was one of the chief causes of the decadence of the Greek Mysteries.

As explained on a previous page, one of the objects of the occultist of the Left-hand Path is to render available and conserve on the Inner Planes the energy generated by sex-force without having to practise self-control and sublimation. Normally, the life-force is brought down from its Divine Source through the positive male vehicle, and returned back to the Source of all Life through the negative female vehicle, thus completing the circuit. If, however, there be no vehicle of the opposite magnetism to form the returning arc, that force is either 'earthed' and diffused, or, if there be the necessary occult knowledge, it is conserved for magical purposes. It is the latter end which is pursued by the individuals we have referred to who inculcate unnatural vice as a means of producing psychic development, which it unquestionably does. With that psychic development, however, goes an irritability of the nervous system which shows itself in excessive sensitiveness and violent outbursts of temper, thus clearly revealing the pathological nature of such development and what poles asunder it is from the trained psychism of the true initiate, who, above all else, shows by his health and serenity the soundness of the system on which he works.

We may finally notice that form of black occultism, less common in England than the others already considered, in which cruelty and blood sacrifice play a part. Any strong emotion is a source of astral energy, and fear and pain are no exceptions to the rule. Moreover, blood, being a vital fluid, contains a large proportion of ectoplasm, or etheric substance. When shed, this ectoplasm rapidly separates from the congealing blood and thus becomes available for materializations; it is for this reason that blood sacrifices are offered to deities of a certain type by primitive peoples. Only the lowest types of entities will use the etheric emanations of blood for their manifestations, higher types use the ethers which are set free when certain volatile substances are burnt, hence the use of incense in magical work.

The evocation of these lower forms of life is a very dangerous undertaking and can only be performed by a very advanced occultist. To evoke such beings for experimental purposes is not legitimate, for in order to materialize, they draw a proportion of etheric substance from each person taking part in the ceremonial. Even when the magic circle be used for protection, some etheric emanation at least has to be extruded across it if full manifestation with function is to take place; and although the entity may be forced to disgorge before being given the licence to depart, the ectoplasm it has used comes back to its owner horribly contaminated.

The only circumstances, in my opinion, under which such an evocation is justifable, is when an exorcism is being performed in order to free a person from the domination of such an entity, and magic has to be called in to undo what magic has already done.

14.

Psychic Pathologies

'Evil is wrought by want of thought as well as by want of heart.' Let us now consider the occult troubles which arise from ignorance and inexperience. These may be divided into three broad divisions: firstly, the troubles which come from hypersensitiveness induced by improper methods of training, or training under unsuitable conditions; secondly, the forming of rapports without the knowledge of the methods of breaking them and resealing the aura; and thirdly, dissociation of the personality through the use of improper methods of psychism, a common trouble with the untrained psychic.

A psychic is always a sensitive. He is sensitive not only to impressions from the Inner Planes, but to every change of feeling in those about him. He is like a person who goes abroad on a treacherous spring day clad in the thinnest of garments and feeling every change of temperature, now chilled by the wind, now scorched by the sun. Such a one experiences constant changes of mood and is torn to pieces by his own emotions. Moreover, he is constantly quarrelling with people, for he is acutely aware of the ups and downs of their feelings towards himself, and a single thought of irritation is to him as a blow in the face. Unless sheltered and cared for with wise and understanding sympathy, the psychic is very apt to become neurotic and end in social disgrace.

Spontaneous natural psychism is the fruit of training undergone in past lives. This training is of two types; it may have been designed to produce the sybil, the watcher of the magical mirror; or it may be the result of initiation and adepthood. The former type gives the passive, negative psychism and is usually found in psychics of little mentality; the latter type has invariably associated with it qualities of mind and character which show the lineage of the soul.

When one who has previously been an initiate has reached the point in this incarnation when he is ready to take the Path again, he is gathered back into his old Order and re-initiated. From that moment no more is heard publicly of his psychism. There are cases, however, in which this does not occur, and one who has obviously been in the Mysteries wanders unshepherded. It will usually be found in such cases that trouble has occurred in the past and that that soul was expelled from his Order for some offence against its ethics. Such souls are often quite well aware of this, and know that occult studies are forbidden to them in this incarnation.

A degree of psychism can be produced in most people by the methods of training which are fairly widely in vogue at present. If the system be sound and the conditions under which it can be followed are suitable, a reliable, even if not very extensive, psychism can be developed. Psychism is like singing; though a large number of people can, with application, learn to be adequate performers for choral work, natural gifts are necessary for its highest achievements.

Whatever system teaches the opening of the higher consciousness should also teach the methods of its closing, for to keep the higher centres open all the time racks the brain-consciousness to pieces. The method of closing is quite simple for anyone who has learned concentration and who has trained the subconscious time-faculty. A time-limit is fixed when consciousness is opened; and just as many people can cause themselves to wake from sleep at a given hour, so the psychic teaches himself to return to normal consciousness at the appointed time. He then concentrates his attention on some mundane occupation and the psychic centres close automatically. This is the reason why craftwork is insisted upon in many forms of occult training. The hour for the use of the hands comes round and the chakras have a rest.

It is for this reason that the Western occultist, and especially such as concentrate the forces with ritual, deprecate vegetarianism when training, especially if the student has to remain out in the world, going about his ordinary business. When the centres are opened with the help of a refining diet, they cannot be closed at will, and unless the neophyte can lead a sheltered life, nervous disturbances ensue. Especially is this the case when, through the injudicious management of the diet or inability to assimilate vegetable proteins, which are much more indigestible than animal proteins, there is malnutrition with all its debilitating effects. Should this occur, as it frequently does, vegetarianism may, of course, be persisted in for humanitarian reasons; the decision is one for each individual conscience and all respect is due to the person who elects to suffer for conscience sake, but under circumstances occult training must be discontinued.

Although certain Eastern systems cannot be pursued without the sensitizing effect of a vegetarian diet, the Western systems, for the most part not only do not depend on diet for their results, but are actually unsuitable for the use of a person who has been so sensitized. The issues between humanitarianism and occultism have been much confused of recent years by modern Theosophical teaching. As a matter of fact, they have no correlation. People may be humanitarians who are not occultists, and occultists who are not humanitarians.

There is a very great difference between the expanded consciousness of the trained occultist and the sensitiveness of the psychic. The former functions positively on the plane of mind; the latter is receptive and negative on the astral plane, which is the plane of the emotions. He is swept backwards and forwards by every astral wind that blows. He is blamed for his treachery, his changeability, his sudden malice; but as a matter of fact he is the victim of circumstances, as little to be blamed as a school-child who catches measles, mumps, scarlet fever, and whooping-cough one after another; the germs were going about, and he was not immune.

The psychic and mystic frequently ask why any training is necessary. They declare that they have got their contacts and their vision; they know that all knowledge and power are within the heart; what more can be added unto them? To this the occultist answers that a knowledge of the technique and psychology of the higher consciousness will enable them to keep that vision unimpaired and protect them from many dangers of which they are unaware and concerning which they may at any moment be rudely enlightened by experience. Occult discipline is to the psychic what the training of his voice is to the singer. Untrained voices, however beautiful, do not last long, and the higher ranges of their art are not possible to them.

His sensitivenss renders the psychic suspicious and quarrelsome, and because he is keenly alive to the unseen forces, he is terribly afraid of black magic. To him, any force which he does not understand and which seems to him to be stronger than himself, is evil. He knows only too well his own extreme suggestibility, and he defends himself from undue influence by a ready suspiciousness and fiery resentment like that of a thoroughbred horse rendered vicious by ill-treatment. With such a suggestible subject, the suspicion of fraud held in the minds of a circle of sitters is enough to make him doubt his own integrity and either totally prevent all manifestation, or cause him to become that which they believe him to be, just as the hypnotized patient, when the doctor says to him, 'You are getting better,' in very truth gets better. This hyper-suggestibility of the psychic is the cause of many of the falls from grace on the part of hitherto genuine mediums which the Press exposes with such gusto.

The untrained psychic, having no general knowledge of esoteric science or of the history of supernatural phenomena, has no standards of comparison by which to judge his own work. To him it is unique, sacred, a divine revelation; whosoever lays a critical finger upon it is guilty of blasphemy. The astral psychic always believes his visions to be spiritual and has a horror of the very word astral. As a matter of fact, all vision is astral; spiritual experiences have no form but are pure idea and intuition. The mistake is made of believing that a change of sub-plane is really a change of plane. There is a wide difference between the lower and higher astral sub-planes; on the higher levels of the astral are the greatest beauty and purity. Nevertheless, they are still astral. The Spiritual Plane is made of sterner stuff, and it is only accessible to those who can first rise through the Concrete and Abstract Mental Planes, and having utilized the mind to the full, transcend it. Any form of visual or auditory consciousness belongs to the planes of form; the higher planes are contacted through pure idea and realization. It is this philosophic concept of esoteric science which it is so necessary to stress at the present time as a counterbalance against the phenomenal, anthropomorphic concept which has been so widely spread about by much propaganda literature on the subject; a state of affairs which is deplored by all serious-minded students of the Ancient Wisdom.

The phenomena connected with rapport are also a fruitful cause of pathology. Rapport is like blood-transfusion, there is an exchange of vitality between the persons concerned. If there be mutual sympathy and good health, rapport is a most valuable and useful thing, for there is reciprocity. The strength of each supplements the weaknesses of the other. The real value of marriage lies in the establishment of rapport on all the planes.

The position is very different, however, when it is a case of all give and no take, or where there is a pathology in one of the partners to a rapport. Vitality is like any other mobile substance; it tends to flow from a centre of high pressure to a centre of low pressure until the pressure is equalized. Most of us only establish a rapport with those with whom we are in close emotional touch, but in the psychic, the ectoplasm often projects long processes beyond the edge of the aura, and rapport is easily established. Where there is a need, the sympathy flows and where the sympathy flows the ectoplasm flows too, and along its tenuous threads goes the vitality. The leaking aura is not at all uncommon, and accounts for much ill health in psychics.

This condition needs careful and prolonged treatment. The rapport must first be broken by a complete severance of all relations for a time if this be possible, and also by certain occult means which cannot be entered upon here. To break the rapport, however, is not enough unless the rents in the aura be closed; the vitality will continue to leak and rapports to be formed with any who are devitalized. This is not a deliberate vampirism, but simply an acute form of the normal interchange of vitality and polarization which goes on all the time between all forms of life.

In order to cause the aura to heal up and strengthen, the physical and mental health must be built up in circumstances of emotional quiet. A return to nature is the best medicine, for nature is a powerful healer for all psychic troubles. The re-establishment of physical health must always go hand in hand with the solution of occult problems. A lowered vitality leaves an open gate to invasion.

Lastly, we come to the point where lies the root of so much occult trouble, the point where psychism and psychopathology meet. The sensitiveness of the psychic can so easily turn into mental instability under adverse circumstances. For its proper understanding a knowledge of psychology is necessary. Whoever wants to understand this subject cannot do better than study *Dream Psychology*, by Maurice Nichol. *The Psychology of Insanity*, by Bernard Hart, is also very illuminating, and my own little book, *Machinery of the Mind* (V. M. Firth), is a general introduction to the subject.

An adequate knowledge of the elements of both normal and abnormal psychology would do more than anything else towards preventing false concepts of occultism. When all is said and done, occultism is simply the science which deals with extended consciousness, and the experiences which that extended consciousness opens up, and unless we have a proper concept of the nature of consciousness, we can never hope to understand occultism. It is so much easier, however, to acquire a rule-of-thumb knowledge of occult phenomena, or alleged phenomena, and human nature is so fond of short cuts which save effort and application, that it is not easy to get would-be students to realize that profound philosophical concepts must be clearly grasped before the occult doctrines can be understood. Apart from these, we get naïve and anthropomorphic concepts of a universe cut out of cardboard—a child's toy theatre of a cosmos; and lucky are we if we get it plain, without the addition of gaudy colourings.

15.

Mental Trespassing

The realization of the power of thought is widespread, and there are many people who not only carefully avoid doing positive harm to others by their wrong thinking, but seek to do active good by their right thinking, and the question arises, how far is one justified in using the power of concentrated thought to help another?

Many people will think this an absurd question. Of course one is justified in doing good, in season and out of season. But the problem is not quite so simple as all that. Let us take a concrete instance which may come close home to us. Supposing someone, who still adheres to the orthodox ways of thinking from which the reader of these pages has presumably broken away, should elect to save your soul from damnation by concentrating on you and giving you telepathic suggestion to the effect that you could not assimilate this line of thought, would you welcome the interference? Would you not rather consider it a most unwarrantable intrusion upon your freedom of action and the integrity of your soul? How, then, do you suppose it might appear to other people if you, even with the best of intentions, sent mental messages to their subconscious mind designed to bring about a change in their condition?

It may be laid down as a maxim in spiritual healing that no one has the right to apply any alterative mental treatment to another without that person's consent. Is it too much to expect that you should write to that person, stating what you propose to do, and obtain his consent before you submit him to a course of treatment? If you have any reason to suspect that such consent might not be forthcoming, is that a justification for giving the treatment without his knowledge? How would you feel about it if such methods were applied to yourself? Supposing you were engaged in some delicate and difficult process of training in order to obtain the higher consciousness, and someone sent concentrated mental messages to you which disturbed your concentration and spoilt your experiment, would you not feel that you had just cause for complaint?

It has been argued that surely anybody would welcome relief from pain. But this is far from being the case. Many people have profound religious convictions, and would consider such interference blasphemous. Even if we do not agree with them, we ought to respect their opinions.

Do not forget that when we concentrate upon another person and thereby effect a rapport, that such a rapport continues after the treatment is finished. Next time we concentrate we shall 'get through' more easily. An interchange of mental content has taken place between mind and mind, and this continues to flow backwards and forwards like the tides through a strait unless there is sufficient understanding of the technique of the operation to know how to 'shut down' at the conclusion of a treatment. Moreover, although the healer may be able to 'shut down' and prevent any emanation of his patient's mind from touching his own consciousness, the patient is not usually in a position to do this in regard to his healer; especially is this the case when the treatment is administered without the knowledge of the patient.

A person who has once had such a rapport established between his subconscious mind and the mind of another will have undergone a marked increase of telepathic sensitiveness, and anyone else will find it much easier to establish a similar rapport. Have we the right to produce this sensitization in anyone without their consent?

Supposing that such an interchange of mental content as we have described takes place between two people whose viewpoint is antagonistic, great confusion and conflict are caused in the mind of the patient. His judgment is clouded and his will deflected from its purpose.

Is there anybody who has sufficient wisdom to know the needs of another soul? They must be judged according to evolutionary development; the particular karmic debt that soul is working out at the moment; its general karmic position, derived from the aggregate of the causes set going in numberless past lives, all interacting among themselves, reinforcing and counteracting each other, some coming into action at one moment, some at another as the planetary conditions influence the individual horoscope. Until you have diagnosed these conditions, you would do well to refrain form operating upon them. If your mental power is sufficient to heal when rightly applied, it is sufficient to make confusion more confounded when wrongly applied.

There is but one safe way to apply spiritual forces impersonally, and that is to invoke God's love and commit the soul to God's hands.

16.

Occultism and Vegetarianism

There has been a great deal of discussion recently concerning the necessity of a meatless diet for an occult student. Members of many different occult schools have taken part in this discussion, which seems to proceed entirely on the deductive method, arguing from first principles which may or may not be conceded by the other participants; no one, so far, appears to have asked, 'What are the actual facts of the case? What has been the practice of those who are recognized as among the masters of the occult art?'

Initiates are divided in this matter; some, like Pythagoras, inculcate a strict vegetarianism; others, like Jesus, said, 'It is not that which goeth in at the mouth which defileth a man, but that which proceeds from the heart.' Of the moderns, Max Heindel was a vegetarian; Rudolf Steiner was not. Dr Besant was a vegetarian; Eliphas Levi was not. The Swami Vivekananda, one of the most advanced teachers of occultism who have ever come to the West from the East, poured scorn on the idea that vegetarian diet could raise consciousness. 'If this were the case', he said— 'Then the cow and the sheep would be the most advanced yogis.' There is evidently, therefore, room for discussion in the matter of the best diet for the occult path, and it cannot be taken as a *sine qua non* that vegetarian is either the best, or the only possible diet.

The discussion of the whole question of vegetarianism can be approached from three separate points of view: the hygienic, the humanitarian, and the occult; and the occult point of view has to take into consideration both the hygienic and the humanitarian. We will consider each of these separately, on their own merits, and then consider them from the occult standpoint.

I was once discussing the question of vegetarianism with a well-known

Harley Street doctor, and he said a thing which impressed me as being the truest word I had yet heard spoken on the subject.

'Most people seem to think,' he said, 'that although there is an infinite variety about our external appearance, our insides are made to a sealed pattern. In my cabinet I have a large collection of X-ray photographs, and I can recognize my different patients by the portraits of their stomachs just as I could by the photographs of their faces. If there is so much divergency in their internal appearances, must there not be an equal divergency in their internal needs?'

Sir Thomas Horder pointed out in an article in the *Lancet* that argument from individual dietetic experience was valueless. A thin, hardworking, neurasthenic type of man would need one kind of diet, and a fat little dilettante with a high blood-pressure would require another. He also quoted the case of a big buxom woman with a delicate dyspeptic husband, who said to him, 'Would it not benefit my husband, doctor, if he were a vegetarian like myself?'

'Madam,' he replied, 'I perceive that you can afford to be a vegetarian.' Risking, as he said, the good lady's wrath by so doing, for it is a curious thing that even those who take up vegetarianism for health reasons, quite apart from humanitarian considerations, seem to make a religion of it, and are willing not only to suffer for their faith, but to persecute for it. Were it not for this attitude, diet reform would be on a very much sounder basis than it is today, for it is not easy to get at the truth when people are willing to pervert it on a question of principle.

Undoubtedly it must be conceded by all reasonable persons that many people have recovered health on a vegetarian diet after all else failed. But the question we here have to consider is, were they cases of physical or psychical illness? And was it the actual diet that restored to health, or their faith in it, and the possession of a new interest in life? Instead of talking of their ill health, to all their friends, they now begin to talk about their good health, and the suspicion might arise that previously they were not nearly as ill as they thought they were, and that now they may not be nearly as well as they think they are. As Sir Thomas Horder remarked, many people are well in spite of their diet fads, and not on account of them, and while we must agree that many people can and do thrive on a vegetarian diet, we must also admit that many do not.

Another point in connection with a meatless diet, a point which has an important bearing upon occult training, is the observed fact that it undoubtedly does lead to increased sensitivity of the nerves. This is the reason why it is advocated as a means of furthering psychic development. Let us remember, however, that there is psychism and psychism. One kind is indeed true soul-vision, but the other is an aberration of the imagination, and to the latter a lowered physical vitality unquestionably predisposes.

I do not mean to imply by this that it is not possible to maintain health on a strict vegetarian diet, but I do maintain that it is not possible for everybody to do so under all circumstances. To take a person accustomed to an ordinary mixed diet, and start him on vegetarian diet and occult training at the same time is rarely satisfactory, especially if that person is engaged in a strenuous or exacting occupation or has difficulty in getting meat substitutes. This is all too often done by teachers of occultism, and it is an exceedingly unwise method of procedure.

This brings us to the next point in our consideration. Should the follower of the Path stick to his vegetarianism whether it suits him or not, and whether he can obtain meat substitutes or not? Some would say yes, and act up to it. But other considerations come into the matter. It is not possible for anyone to follow the strenuous experiences of a genuine occult training unless he is in good health. The Path is no place for a weakling, as many a one has found to his cost. Equally, if a person sticks rigidly to his vegetarianism in spite of all drawbacks, is he to be admitted to an occult training regardless of his physical condition? No occult teacher worthy of the name would do so.

There are, in my experience, an instability and lack of ballast among faddists of all ways of thinking which do not form a good foundation for that study of all others which requires a level head and an iron nerve. Extremes have never been a success in any walk of life. One might define the crank as a man who cannot see the wood for one solitary tree against which he has glued his nose. If the highest ideals are not governed by a sense of proportion, that man's work for humanity will be 'out of the true', will, in fact, be 'cranky' in the literal sense of the word.

I am afraid that I have a constitutional dislike of any extremes of any sort, and I believe that it is better to 'see life steadily and see it whole' than attempt one-sided reforms. The more I see of the occult world, the more I deplore the general absence of an impartial and scientific attitude. The question of diet should be approached from the standpoints of physiology and psychology as well as from that of idealism, especially in view of the fact that different teachers differ in their ideals.

The question of vegetarianism from the humanitarian standpoint is also an extremely vexed question, and not nearly so simple as its advocates would have us believe. The whole issue must depend upon our attitude towards the domestication of animals. Was it wrong to domesticate them? Are domestic animals essential to civilization? If we admit that the exploitation of one natural kingdom by another is fundamentally wrong, people of sensitive conscience will feel it incumbent upon them to refrain from participating in that exploitation. But the exploitation consists of much more than flesh-eating. The wearing of leather boots and bone buttons, the use of glue, size, hair, and a thousand other of the by-products of animal life have to be considered. Every time we hold on by a strap in a train, we are availing ourselves of the products of animal slaughter. This argument, is, of course, a *reductio ad absurdum*, and shows that the advocacy of vegetarian diet cannot safely be pursued along these lines.

As long as we have the domestication of animals, we shall have their slaughter at the hands of man, even if that slaughter be the merciful despatch of the aged and diseased, or the destruction of superfluous males. Unless we are prepared to take our stand for the total abolition of animal domestication, we shall never get away from the taking of animal life.

Do the Brethren of the Great White Lodge, under whom all occultists take their initiations and to whom they look as teachers and Masters, require that their pupils should refrain from having any participation in the taking of life in any form? We know that some of the Eastern schools do so teach for the Jain priests carry a soft broom with them and gently sweep the path before them as they walk lest they should accidentally tread on some creeping thing and take its life. We also know that certain Indian ascetics refused to remove maggots from their sores, even going to the length of replacing them when they fell off, saying, 'I would not inconvenience thee, brother.' Such an attitude has never found favour in the West. The mediaeval saints, like Blessed Henry Suso, did not refrain from cleanliness lest it should be the occasion of discomfort to their vermin, but lest it should be the occasion of comfort to themselves.

What, then, should be our attitude as practical seekers after the Light, coming to it by a Western Path? I do not think we can find a better model than our Lord and Master. He was indeed the Master of Compassion but He was no sentimentalist, neither was He in any way a crank. It has always been noteworthy that He never inculcated any extreme form of humanitarianism, but rather a compassionate attitude towards all things, great and small. Out of such an attitude right relationships with the animal kingdom must come, just as right relations with the human kingdom must come. But just as we are not yet in sight of the abolition of war and prisons and the burden laid upon man of earning his bread in the sweat of his brow, so we are not within sight of the abolition of animal domestication, and all that inevitably goes with it. The abolition of unnecessary suffering is undoubtedly incumbent upon us, but as long as domestic animals are with us it is hardly possible to give them a greater share in the amenities of life than human beings enjoy.

In considering all practical problems, especially those which have to be worked out on a large scale, it is not possible always to find out the abstract right, and then go and do it. We often have to be content with what is practicable at the moment, or even the lesser of two evils.

There will always be sensitive people who, when they realize the suffering that goes to the production of some of the food we eat and the clothes we wear, will refuse to partake of that food or wear those clothes because they are so keenly alive to that suffering. No one can say that this is other than a noble sacrifice that they are making, but do the Masters require this sacrifice of their pupils as a condition of acceptance? That is our problem as practical occultists. The answer lies in the fact that not all initiates have been abstainers from the use of animal products, therefore obviously such abstention is not a *sine qua non* of occult work, even though it may be a specific requirement of certain occult schools.

There are two ways of obtaining perception of a subtle vibration, either by focussing and magnifying the vibrations, or by increasing the sensitivity of the receiving instrument. Some occult schools use the latter method, and therefore they eschew the use of meat in order to obtain the great nervous sensitivity which a meatless diet undoubtedly does produce, although there is a serious reason to believe that this sensitivity is of the same type as is produced by a prolonged fast, and is really the temporarily heightened mental activity due to malnutrition. It has been the practice of most occult and mystic schools to induce a temporary exaltation of consciousness by abstention, and such practices, rightly employed, are undoubtedly part of the system of occult training as practised by all races; but the wise occultist realizes that such a heightening can be but temporary, and that there is a price to pay for these practices. He may decide, and quite legitimately, that the gain is worth the price, but there comes a point when the price becomes extortionate, and if he be wise, he will not push his abstinence, whether from stimulating foods or from food itself, beyond the point where the price outweighs the gain. His aim, as an occultist, is the exaltation of consciousness for the sake of the experience so gained, not the salvation of the animal kingdom.

This is the point where clear thinking is needed. In abstention from flesh foods, is the occultist motivated by humane ideals or a desire for knowledge through the exaltation of consciousness which follows on abstinence? And if the latter, to what point can he carry that abstinence without impairing his health? The answer to this question must be entirely individual because individuals vary so enormously in their stamina and dietetic needs. One thing is quite certain, that a man in a poor state of health is as little likely to succeed on the Occult Path as he is in any other exacting vocation.

To sum up, my judgment in the matter would be that a restricted diet is used by certain schools of occult training in order to produce enhanced sensitiveness. Such a method is satisfactory provided that the person thus rendered sensitive can be sheltered from the shocks and buffets of life; otherwise it is a disastrous method to pursue. It is a method which is seldom successful in the West because the Western constitution is not easily rendered sensitive, and therefore devitalization has to be carried to considerable lengths before it becomes effective, and the line between refinement and debilitation is hard to draw. This method is especially undesirable for anyone who is leading the ordinary life of the world and is obliged to work under the pressure of modern city conditions; it is rendered additionally difficult by our cold and variable climate. If, however, a student elects to enroll in an occult school which uses this dietetic method, he would naturally have to adhere to the discipline he has chosen. I therefore do not advocate the use of these methods in the West because I have seldom observed them to be satisfactory as a means of opening up the higher consciousness among Europeans (I would ask it to be noted that I do not include astral psychism under the term higher consciousness), and it very frequently produces a debility which renders any form of efficient work impossible.

The advice that was given to me by my own teacher I believe to be sound: 'Follow the customs of the country in which you are domiciled, and thereby enter sympathetically into the life of its group-soul. Be, however, on the abstemious side; do not indulge the flesh, but do not estrange yourself from the group-life by eccentricities and affectations.' The occultist needs to keep himself physically fit for his exacting work. If he prefers a vegetarian diet by reason of taste or conscience, by all means let him have it. There is no objection to vegetarianism as a diet so long as it is giving satisfactory results. The thing against which the common-sense student of occult science must set his face is the elevation of vegetarianism into a fetish, and the persistence in it when, owing either to personal idiosyncrasies or circumstances, it has proved a failure.

In view of the fact that so many of our greatest initiates have been flesh-eaters, it is useless to argue that vegetarianism is an essential upon the Path, for obviously it cannot be, or they would not have been initiated.

The person with the sensitive conscience and the vivid imagination will no doubt eschew flesh-foods because of his feelings in the matter, and his scruples are entitled to respect, as is all sincerity; but as sane occultists we must deny the contention that vegetarianism is a *sine qua non* of occult development. We must also draw attention to the fact that the results of it are very often entirely negative from the occult point of view and extremely unsatisfactory from the health point of view. Let those who wish to be vegetarians for whatever reason, humane or dietetic, have the liberty to be vegetarians, and if their health under such circumstances permits, follow any pursuit that seems good to them; but let us frankly face the fact that occult development, for the man of Western race at any rate, is not dependent upon any particular diet so long as that diet is healthful, and let us once and for all explode the idea that only a vegetarian can be an initiate, for the facts show us that this is not the case.

Occult science needs to rely more on an appeal to facts and less on appeals to first principles which may very well be fanciful. It has not yet freed itself from the trammels of the Middle Ages, and still uses pre-Baconian methods, depending on argument and authorities rather than on observation and experimentation. I have been much struck by the fact that in the vegetarian controversy which raged at one time in the pages of the *Occult Review*, no one appealed to experience, which would have revealed the undoubted fact that meat-eaters were among the greatest of the world's occultists.

I hold strongly the belief that we can only base our civilization on an ethical basis, but I hold equally strongly the belief that that ethic has to be sane and practical, and that the right way is usually half-way between two extremes. I deprecate the use of *pâté de foie gras* and ospreys, and equally I deprecate the Eastern ascetic with his broom and his maggots. Likewise I deprecate the attitude of mind that repudiates the use of fur but accepts the use of leather.

I also have my doubts of the idealist who does not find the teaching of the Gospels sufficiently lofty for his needs.

17.

Eastern Methods and Western Bodies

Many people think that the East is the only home of occultism, but this is far from being the case. Every race has had, and still has, its traditional, guarded wisdom, revealed to the few and concealed from the many. Our own Western tradition traces its origin to Egypt, with tributaries from Chaldea, Greece, and the fierce Norse tradition. It comes down to us through the Qabalists and Alchemists, and it is alive and active at the present day.

Strange as it may appear, it is the Eastern tradition, its methods and terminology that are most generally known among us, and for two reasons. Firstly, because the Western Tradition has always been, and still is, very guarded and secretive in its methods; whether rightly or wrongly is a matter of opinion. There is much to be said both for and against secrecy in occultism. And secondly, the Theosophical Society, whose methods and contacts are Eastern, has over fifty years of active propaganda work to its credit.

It may not unreasonably be asked why it was, if there were an active esoteric tradition in Europe, that Mme Blavatsky, the founder of the Theosophical Society, did not take her initiation in its schools instead of having to seek her Master in the East. The explanation is a simple ethnological one. The Russians, according to the old saying, are not the most Easterly of the Westerns, but the most Westerly of the Easterns. One has only to look at the portraits of Mme Blavatsky to see the Tartar blood and to realize that her affinities would be with the Light of Asia.

The principles taught in all the great racial traditions are the same, but the different traditions have brought different aspects of esoteric science to a high degree of development according to the natural inclination of racial temperament. The pagan faiths of the West developed the nature contacts. Modern Western occultism rising from this basis, seems to be taking for its field the little-known powers of the mind. The Eastern tradition has a very highly developed metaphysics. We do well to study these different aspects where we find them in their highest degree of development. The Sacred Books of the East and the popular expositions thereof are invaluable to the Western occultist. Nevertheless, when it comes to the practial application of these principles and especially the processes of occult training and initiation, it is best for a man to follow the line of his own racial evolution. It is very seldom that a European, living in Europe, is successfully trained by Eastern methods. If a man or woman is able to go to the East and completely sink themselves in the Eastern group-soul it is possible for them to go a certain way in the Eastern tradition, but we have no record of any European reaching the higher degrees.

The reason for the inadvisability of an alien initiation does not lie in racial antagonism, nor in any failure to appreciate the beauty and profundity of the Eastern systems, but for the same reason that Eastern methods of agriculture are inapplicable in the West—because conditions are different.

As has already been said, different schools develop different aspects of occult science. These aspects are developed not only according to racial temperament, but also according to racial Darma, or duty. When a nation has a particular task to fulfil, the initiates of that nation give a lead along the destined lines. The esoteric discipline which enabled the Hindu race to develop the higher mind would not only have been inapplicable to the Anglo-Saxon race whose task it was to develop the concrete mind, but would actually have prevented that development from taking place because it is necessary to close down the higher consciousness if the lower consciousness is to be operated. The two methods would be mutually antagonistic and destructive, and yet they were right for those to whom they belonged; nevertheless, each of the races, different as is their destiny, can profit by the achievements of the other, for qualities and faculties once brought through into manifestation on this earth belong to humanity as a whole and form part of the common heritage to which each race in turn brings its gifts—Beauty from Greece, Order from Rome, Spiritual Philosophy from India.

There will always be individuals in every race who feel that their spiritual home is elsewhere, but they are exceptional. There will never be many Richard Burtons or Sadhu Sundar Singhs in a race. For the most part they will be Smiths and McGregors and Murpheys. But although there will always be individual exceptions, no one seeking the Ancient Wisdom should be encouraged to follow an alien tradition unless he has a very definite bias in that direction, for even when there is a definite spiritual affinity with the East, the problem of training a Western body by Eastern methods presents many difficulties. The study of such books as those of the Swami Vivekananda, in which the Yogi methods are very plainly set forth, reveals the fact that the opening of the higher centres of consciousness according to the Eastern methods depends on the re-directing of the etheric currents in the physical body, and the concentrating of them upon certain centres known as the chakras.

If we study the anatomy of the subject, we shall see that these chakras correspond with the endocrine glands, and that the changes in consciousness are brought about by producing changes in the chemical composition of the blood by checking or stimulating the different ductless glands. Western physiology is beginning to wake up to the intimate connection between the ductless glands and the mind, and is studying them in connection with those changes of consciousness known as insanity, and there is no doubt at all as to the intimate connection between the endocrines (or chakras) and the mind. The ancient Eastern Tradition is confirmed in its doctrine by Western experimental science.

But here comes the rub from the point of view of the seeker after initiation. The endocrine balance in different races differs profoundly. It is this difference which produced the different racial types; this is proved by the fact that if we get a disturbance of the endocrine balance in childhood, we shall get a Mongolian, or even a negroid appearance in a child of pure European stock. Such a child, however, will be a diseased and sub-normal individual, because the other endocrine secretions have not been modified proportionately, as they are in the case of the normal Chinese or negro, whose endocrines are balanced according to type. It is quite true that other branches of the Aryan stock are nearer akin to us than these other root-races, but the pigmentation of the skin, and the structure of the skeleton reveal fundamental variations. We have only to realize the difference in resistance to shock between the Hindu, the Anglo-Saxon, and the negro, to realize that different initiatory methods would have to be used with them. The Hindu dies readily from shock, pure and simple. The Anglo-Saxon will be upset by it, but he is exceedingly unlikely to die of it. And as for the negro, he is practically immune. It follows therefore that the methods to which the sensitive Hindu will respond will, under normal conditions, have as little effect on the other two as water on a duck's back, and the methods which suit the negro would shatter the white man.

In order to become a suitable subject for Eastern methods, an Anglo-

Saxon has to undergo a long period of sensitization. At the end of that period he may be fitted for an Eastern initiation, but he is quite unfitted for a Western life. In very few cases is a successful issue arrived at.

The Western initiatory method consists in strengthening, not sensitizing the candidate, and then concentrating the subtle forces by means of a ritual. A man thus trained, far from being unfitted for the struggle for existence in the rush and drive of modern life, has acquired stamina quite out of the ordinary, and is distinguished by his powers of endurance and ability to control the reactions of his body, resisting cold, hunger, and pain in a remarkable degree. This, of course, is equally true of the Eastern adept; he also has dominion over the elements in his own nature. There are many well-authenticated accounts of the feats of endurance of those trained in the Ancient Wisdom of the East. There is nothing in the occult discipline, rightly applied, which is going to make invalids or nervous wrecks of its students; it is, apparently, the application of methods designed for one type of physique, social organization and climate, to individuals of another racial and social order which gives such unsatisfactory results and produces the weedy-looking neurotics so common in esoteric circles.

Whatever argument may be adduced concerning the brotherhood of man, experience proves that the spiritual methods of one racial type seldom suit another. If the ethnological map of Europe be compared with the map showing the distribution of the different religious systems, it will immediately become apparent that the boundary lines are identical. Catholic Christianity coincides with the geographical distribution of the Latin races; Protestant Christianity coincides with the Nordic populations.

In neither Asia nor Africa is the missionary's convert considered a desirable employee. 'A native converted is a native spoiled,' is a proverb in two different continents.

Such observations as these confirm the tradition that the Great White Lodge gives to each race the religion suited to its needs. It is the esoteric and mystical side of each religion which forms the initiatory school of its race. Unless a man has had the elementary training of a tradition he is unlikely to profit by its advanced work. To grow up under the discipline of exoteric Christianity and then suddenly go on to a school of esoteric Buddhism without first being received into the Buddhist faith is like working for the intermediate B.A. and then wanting to proceed to the final B.Sc. Still more do such considerations apply to the Hindu esoteric tradition, wherein the greatest importance is attached to physical considerations, such as heredity, diet, and contacts. To take up Yogi systems while disregarding these things is mere occult amateurism; no

Asiatic would take such a person seriously.

The Eastern guru is especially at a disadvantage in dealing with Western women because the Eastern and Western attitudes towards women differ so widely. Equally is he at a disadvantage in counselling his male pupils concering such matters as marriage and their relations with women in general. The management of the sex forces is an exceedingly important things in occultism, and attitudes towards sex in the East and in the West are poles asunder. The Eastern teacher may be able to instruct his pupils in philosophy, but he can give little practical help in matters of ethics, for the subtler aspects of the inner life of a race are a closed book to an alien.

Equally do these considerations apply to Western occult systems transplanted to America. They never strike their roots there, but remain superficial and academic. There is a certain aspect of occult work which has to make use of the magnetism of the land itself. Native systems of magic are built up on this basis and have a technique for its use; alien systems, transplanted, have no such technique, and therefore fail to complete their operations; or, alternatively, should they succeed in contacting the elemental forces of the land, experience much difficulty in keeping them under control and returning them to their proper place when the operation is finished.

American occultism will never come into its own until it ceases to import its systems from Europe and India, but goes back along the line of its own tradition, picking up the aboriginal contacts, and daring to bend them to its own evolutionary purposes. It must seek the contacts of the Sun Temple of Atlantis through the Maya tradition. Egypt has no message for the United States. Americans can learn esoteric philosophy and science from the Western tradition, just as Europeans can learn from the Eastern tradition, but the initiatory forces cannot be conveyed across the Atlantic or the Pacific. Some day there will come an American who will pick up the ancient Maya contacts, adapt them to modern needs, and express their forces in an initiatory ritual which shall be valid for the civilization to which he belongs.

18.

Standards of Judgment

When the seeker after truth has come to the conclusion that occult science gives the explanation of life which satisfies his reason, and that the Way of Initiation is the ideal which satisfies his soul, what is his next step to be? He has a wide choice of literature on the subject, not all of which has the same viewpoint, though upon essentials it is substantially in agreement. He is surrounded by an innumerable company of esoteric organizations, all competing for his adherence. Once received into these circles, he will come in touch with numerous individuals who claim to be able to train and initiate him. What should be his attitude towards all these? He will not have advanced far upon the occult path before he is aware of his need of a teacher. All the books tell him that initiation is essential to his progress beyond a certain point; how is he to obtain that initiation, and how, above all, is he to know which of the societies offering it to him is able to perform that which it promises?

In the pursuit of his occult studies, and in the selection of a teacher, to whom, at the outset he must give his adherence and whose discipline he must accept, the seeker after initiation needs to look for three thin.gs— firstly, right principles: secondly, genuine knowledge: and, thirdly, such common sense and capacity as shall prevent a teacher from involving his pupils in muddles and misadventures.

How is the pupil to test his prospective teacher for these things? Furthermore, is he entitled to test him? I have heard would-be teachers most indignant at the idea of being tested by their pupils. They declare that the recognition of their status is the first test the pupil has to pass; if he is sufficiently intuitive to be worth training, he will see what they are on the inner planes without need to investigate their records on the outer plane.

This is all very well, and may be true enough so far as it goes; but there is absolutely no reason why the pupil should not confirm his psychism, provided he has any, by investigation on the physical plane. Moreover, it is hardly fair to ask of an untrained beginner in occultism that he should trust to his psychism in a matter of such serious import as the selection of a teacher into whose hands he is to commit himself; for although no actual oath of obedience may be required, the fact remains that for all practical purposes the neophyte is pretty much in the hands of his initiator at the outset, and if the senior occultist's power is abused, the neophyte is in for an unpleasant experience, to say the least of it. The true initiator will no more exercise undue influence over his pupil nor abuse his superior knowledge than will the honourable doctor over his patient nor the honourable lawyer over his client; but there are black sheep in every profession, and the occult world, unfortunately, is not sufficiently organized to permit of its black sheep being officially deprived of their power to practise. Therefore the would-be pupil has to look to himself pretty sharply, especially in his early days before he 'knows the ropes.'

The reputable occult teacher, who has nothing to fear from the examination of his record, has no reason to object to having it examined. He ought to be prepared to answer the questions of the person who is proposing to entrust his spiritual advancement and mental welfare into his hands. Why should he not tell a genuine pupil how he received his training, the nature of his contacts, and the source of his financial support? It is only reasonable discretion on the part of a prospective pupil to make such enquiries; to neglect to make them would imply carelessness and lack of discrimination and ordinary common sense.

It may be taken as axiomatic that the person who has nothing to conceal does not resent being investigated. The student has a right to ask questions, and ought to turn down unhesitatingly the teacher who cannot or will not give a satisfactory answer.

The question of money is one that looms large on the horizon at this point of the quest. It is an axiom of occult science that no price may be charged for any form of occult work.

It may generally be presumed that the teacher who has his price and sticks to it is exceedingly unlikely to be an initiator of the Right-hand Path.

On the other hand, we must remember that a teacher or society is certainly entitled to make a sufficient charge to cover the expenses in which it may be involved. Printers will not work for nothing, and lecture rooms have to be heated, cleaned, and owned by someone. It is certainly reasonable to make a charge for value given on the physical plane because somebody is out of pocket in respect of it. Pretty moderate charges, however, will usually cover the actual running expenses of any movement. There ought to be no fee in connection with occult work which it is more convenient to pay by cheque than by coin of the realm.

Another problem, however, comes up in this respect. The occult teacher has to live, and if he has no private means, must either follow some remunerative pursuit, or live by his occult work. If that work is sufficiently extensive to make considerable demands on his time, he must either curtail his work or give up his profession. Under such circumstances, is the occultist justified in allowing his esoteric work to support him? Yes, if it is done in the right way. If he clearly and obviously never permits his remuneration to become a money-making affair, but simply a means of support in order that he may pursue his work, and a very modest means of support at that.

The seeker after initiation must recognize that his teacher has to pay the butcher, the baker, and the candlestick maker, and not unreasonably demand that he should have private means or live on air, but he may justifiably have his doubts of the adept whose pupils appear to find him an expensive pet.

It is very necessary also that the seeker should assure himself of the purity and cleanliness of an occult school. Occultism, as has been pointed out in a previous chapter, is not infrequently used as a cloak for sordid irregularities. The occult forces, especially when concentrated by ritual, unless thoroughly understood and properly controlled, do undoubtedly act as stimulants to the baser aspects of human nature—self-aggrandizement and lust. Human nature in bulk is at best a doubtful commodity, but when it is submitted unregenerate to the powerful stimulation of occult forces, it is apt to be a highly explosive one.

The seeker can form a concept of the purity of a school from the character and conduct of its leading members. What type of person wins advancement in this school? If he observes intelligence and int grity among its more prominent supporters, he may conclude that the inner workings of its organizations are satisfactory.

It will be noted that the qualities for which he is instructed to look are very mundane virtues. Spirituality, devotion, psychism, occult powers—are not reckoned among the qualities by which the true occult school is known. Why is it the seeker is counselled not to look for the things which he most desires to find? For two reasons; firstly, because these things are so easily simulated; and, secondly, because the possessors of the higher spiritual qualities do not wear their hearts on their sleeves for daws to peck at, and the person who goes off into unexpected trances in public is more likely to be an epileptic than an adept.

All phenomena are most carefully guarded by the genuine occultist, and he will only exhibit his powers to people who have won his confidence. In any case, the power to perform phenomena, though it is a proof of knowledge, is no proof of integrity. A man may be a very great psychic and also a very great rascal. There is no correlation between occult powers and spirituality. The thing which is really of value in occult science is not the power to perform marvels or receive wonderful experiences, but the insight into the significance of life and the universe which its teachings give, and the power which its disciplines possess to raise the mind to spiritual realizations. If we look upon occultism as a means to spiritual ends, not magical ends, we shall obtain a true perspective. The psychic phenomena are incidental, a by-product of the real work. This is the distinction by which the initiator weeds out his pupils. He knows that the person whose interest centres in the marvellous will never make a serious student. Therefore he will not be inclined to attract a prospective pupil by an exhibition of phenomena because he knows that the kind of person who would be attracted by such an exhibition is not the kind of person who is going to be any good to him as a student. The occultist who exhibits phenomena indiscriminately is either too ignorant to be aware of the signficance of what he is doing, or too unscrupulous to care.

With regard to the assessment of the actual knowledge which a teacher may possess, the seeker must again fall back upon the test of considering the calibre of the senior students by whom he sees the adept surrounded. He himself, as an outsider, is not in a position to form any first-hand opinion, because the more an occultist knows, the less communicative he is apt to be. The best way of forming an opinion, therefore, is to consider the type of pupil who is passing into the higher degrees. Are they people of outstanding intellectual and spiritual quality? For remember, spirituality alone will not take a man far in the Mysteries; he must have intellectual powers as well. If one sees numbers of well-meaning and enthusiastic ladies of the lecture-room tramp type being advanced to the higher degrees, one can be pretty certain that those higher degrees do not contain anything worth having.

It is also a bad sign to see a teacher without pupil-teachers assisting him. If he is operating a genuine initiatory system, he will have pupils coming along who are on the way to becoming adepts on their own account, and of whose services he is only too glad to avail himself in order to lighten his own burden and extend his work. But where the leader is like a star and dwells apart, one of two things is certain—either he has no system by means of which he can advance his pupils grade by grade, or he is of so jealous a disposition that he will not impart any real knowledge to anybody lest he should be raising up rivals. In such case he is of little use as a teacher.

It is also exceedingly necessary to be cautious in entering into associations with a teacher who is known to be interested in political activities. Those who desire to form an organization for a purpose which they desire to conceal have from time immemorial found in the occult system of organization a convenient cloak for their purpose. To be involved in such an organization is to lay oneself open to considerable unpleasantness. In my opinion, anyone who is taking a prominent position in any spiritual movement ought, in fairness to his followers, to leave politics alone. It is not right to ask people to eat their politics and religion off the same plate.

Then, again, it may be asked, why should common sense and reasonable capacity in the affairs of life be regarded as one of the signs by which to test a teacher? It is well known that the spiritually minded man is often a child in worldly matters. Do not let us forget, however, that there is a great difference between unworldly unsuspiciousness and muddle-headedness, and we can see the two types well exemplified in the Vicar of Wakefield and Mrs Jellaby; the concern of the latter for the natives of Boriboola-ga being such, according to Dickens, that she paid no attention to the yells of her own offspring whose head was jammed in the banisters.

Quite apart from the general confusion, discomfort, and quarrels which are inevitable in the organization of an unpractical teacher, things which effectually prevent any steady work from being accomplished, there is a real danger in handling big occult forces in conditions of emotional disturbance; it is quite likely to lead to at least temporary unbalance. Unless a teacher has sufficient knowledge of the management of the mind to be able to make his own mind function efficiently, he is exceedingly unlikely to be able to guide his pupils safely through the difficult phases of occult development when the mind is 'changing gear' from one type of consciousness to another. Occult training ought to produce a clarification of consciousness and heightening of the powers. If any system produces a general uncoordination and neurotic conditions, it is a thing to be avoided.

A sound and true system of initiation shows itself on the mundane plane in the harmonious ordering of all things. If an adept is himself in confusion and distress, will it not be a blind leading of the blind when he seeks to teach the deeper understanding of life and its laws?

There is another point upon which the seeker is often perplexed, and which it is as well to consider in order that a clear understanding may be arrived at. He has already been counselled to judge an occult school by its senior students: what opinion ought he to form from the statements of those of its members who, for one reason or another, have left it dissatisfied? Here, again, he must exercise caution and common sense. On the one hand he does not want to disregard warnings and involve himself in unpleasantness, and, on the other, he does not want to be put off something which, although it might not have proved suitable for the person who warns him, nevertheless might be of great value to himself.

He must also remember that one story only holds good till the other is told, and that when he has heard the pupil's explanation of his reason for leaving, he has only heard half the tale. He has still to hear the teacher's opinion of the pupil before he is in a position to come to a judgment. The person accustomed to sifting evidence does not judge so much by the tale that is told as by the manner of its telling, and experience proves that the statement that is made with heat and bitterness ought to be corroborated before it is believed.

There are various reasons for which a person may cease to be a member of an occult school, and the enquirer, if he is shrewd and observant, can usually form a pretty good opinion as to which was operative in the case of the person before him.

People shake the dust of an occult school from off their feet for other reasons than because it fails to come up to their expectation. They shake it off with even more emphasis when they fail to come up to its expectations.

There are also many reasons why even apparently right-principled persons bear false witness. Many people try experiments in practical occultism without the slightest realization of what it really is, and, disregarding the instructions of their teacher, burn their fingers. Cases also occur wherein people volunteer to assist in some difficult and dangerous occult undertaking, such as the hunting of a black magician, and at the critical moment their nerve fails them. Are these people going to admit that their courage was not equal to their curiosity? They have to account for their defection somehow, and the more bitterly conscious they are of their own failure, the more bitter will be their denunciations of the leader they have 'let down.'

We must also remember that there is a good deal of mental unbalance in our modern society, and that nothing causes it to flare up quicker than any attempt at practical occultism.

Occultism is a mine of rich ore which well repays the working, and the fact that much of it requires smelting and refining should not deter us from the task. It is no pursuit, however, for the unstable-minded, the ignorant, and the credulous. Three things are necessary for its safe pursuit—a livng spiritual faith, a level head, and a sound knowledge of the psychology of the subconscious mind.

19.

The Ideals of Occultism

In these pages I have repeatedly pointed out the dangers and pitfalls of occultism, but to point out the weaknesses of a movement is insufficient for its remedying, and I would like to put before my readers what I conceive to be the true ideals and aims of occult science.

There is a great difference between the motives which prompt many investigators of the subject and the ideals which are held by those whom their fellow workers would consider to be true leaders of occult thought. Occultism is more than a science or philosophy, it is a religion, and its secrets are not penetrated by study alone, but by dedication. The character as well as the intellect is the instrument of occult investigation; but, in contradistinction to mysticism, in which the character alone may be the instrument and intellectual qualifications do not necessarily enter, occultism requires certain powers of the mind as well as qualities of character for its pursuit. In other words, purification and dedication of character can bring us to the point where the Mystic Christ reveals Itself, but certain additional qualifications of the intellect are necessary for the pursuit of occult science.

Many students attempt the pursuit of occult science by virtue of intellectual qualifications alone, but these, on the one hand, can never hope to penetrate its deeper mysteries, wherein the occult powers lead up to the mystic revelation; and, on the other hand, are liable to certain very serious pathologies of the psychic life, among which hypertrophy of the ego is one of the commonest.

There is only one true path to Initiation and that is the path laid down by immemorial tradition and beaten by countless feet. This path in its earlier stages is different for each of the great races of mankind, but these converging paths finally unite into one broad highway after the Outer

Gate is passed. This Way of Initiation is not a mundane organization, but is a psychic method of leading to spiritual attainment. No society or fraternity has a monopoly of its teachings, neither has any of them the power to convey the full range of its Initiations. Mundane organizations vary enormously in both their power and their purity. They can never be more than a means to an end, an association for mutual help and comradeship. We make a vital mistake if we look upon any system of training as conferring Initiation; only the great Initiator, Whoever or Whatever that may be, can confer Initiation, and all human systems, whether of training or ritual, can only prepare consciousness for His coming.

We choose our occult school in the hope that it may give us guidance and protection on the Path, and we affiliate ourselves thereto with ritual in order that we may become partakers of the ancient Mystery Tradition. This tradition is of very great value, but it is not indispensable; and while it is in the power of occult Orders to convey it, it is not in their power to withhold it, for it is possible for the seeker to rise in consciousness to the Temple not built with hands and there to receive Initiation while out of the body. Such an achievement is rare, and the training and comradeship afforded by a worthy fraternity are of the greatest value to students.

Each occult school has its own ideals, its own methods, its own aims, and, needless to say, its own drawbacks and limitations. Human institutions, like human beings, are finite and imperfect. To its temple we bring our own ideals, and according to the consonance between what we bring with us and what we find there, will be the harmony or otherwise of our relations with that organization. If our ideals be not sufficiently lofty, we shall learn by bitter experience what are the consequences of occultism pursued by wrong means. If our own ideals be loftier than those of the organization with which we have allied ourselves, if our intuitions are a truer guide than our teacher, we shall soon find that the way opens up for us from the Inner Planes, as we make within ourselves the conditions that entitle us to our advancement.

The schools of the true occult tradition train pupils solely in order that those pupils may the better be enabled to serve God. They do not teach their secret methods of extending consciousness and acquiring dominion over the Unseen to enquirers prompted by curiosity and ambition. To such the doors of all reputable organizations are closed, and all those who truly care for the welfare of their fellow men will be thankful that this is the case.

The true occultist holds his knowledge as a sacred trust which he guards for the safety as well as the benefit of his race. He accepts and trains his pupils in order that they may share with him in that trust, and he accepts none as pupils whom he does not believe to be worthy of the confidence he reposes in them; and even after acceptance, he tests them carefully to ensure their fidelity to the great responsibility upon which they are entering. The true occult secrets have never been betrayed in their entirety. In fact, it is only the lesser secrets that are capable of betrayal; the higher secrets of the mystical consciousness are incapable of betrayal because they are not communicated, but realized. Therefore it is that occultists of the Left-hand Path invariably rely upon drugs for the productions of supernormal states of consciousness, and do not attempt the purely psychic methods which are employed by the disciplines of the Right-hand Path. The higher powers of the spirit can only be obtained by the purified consciousness, and therefore are inaccessible to the undedicated and unsanctified.

The adept who is the servant of the Great Initiator looks first for qualities of character in his pupil, and where he finds these, is prepared to give the occult training, provided the mentality of the pupil is such as to enable him to benefit by it. He trains that pupil with a view to service, the service to which he himself is dedicated. That service has various subdivisions, and a brief account of them may be of interest, for it enables us to understand the qualities which are required of the candidate for Initiation. Because a student enters upon one line of activity, however, it does not necessarily mean that he will be concerned with no other, for these activities are as integrally connected as the work of anatomy and physiology. But special aptitudes are required for the different branches of the work, and specialization is therefore temperamental.

The most widely spread section of the initiate's work is concerned with the task of giving expression on the plane of matter and in racial life to those ideals which he has realized when his consciousness has been raised to a higher plane. It is by this means that evolution takes place on the planes of human consciousness. The Logoidal Mind (i.e. the Consciousness of the Solar Logos of this universe, which is not the same thing as the Great Unmanifest, the Root of all Being) is constantly evolving new ideas, and these ideas are perceived intuitively by the exalted consciousness of those great Beings who have advanced beyond our human evolution and no longer incarnate in matter. Co-operating with Them in Their work are those we know as the Lesser Masters, and it is with these that the occultist is especially concerned, for it is they who train him and who expect his co-operation in return for the training given. In fact, they train him solely in order that he may be able to co-operate with them, and therefore dedication to the service of the Masters is the essential preliminary to acceptance as a pupil by them.

These accepted and dedicated pupils are given the training in psychism which enables them to communicate directly with the Masters under whom they work, and they are then employed in the task of relaying through to human life the archetypal ideas which the Lesser Masters have received from the Greater Masters, and which These have in turn perceived in the Logoidal Consciousness. The pupil of the Masters is therefore the earthward end of a living chain of consciousness which is employed in translating the archetypal ideas of the Logos down the planes and finally bringing them to realization in matter.

This can only be achieved by a soul which actually puts them into practice in human life. Many of these will be martyred by their fellow men, unready for such advancements, but their place is immediately filled by others, and so the Divine Impulse fails not. The archetypal ideas, by being thus lived out on the plane of matter, are implanted in the group-mind of the race, and fructify in succeeding generations. It is interesting to note that none but members of a race can implant archetypal ideas successfully in its group-mind. The alien may give the instruction, but it is the native who has to perform the task; hence the failure of missionary efforts unless the ideals presented can inspire the soul of a race.

Millions of souls are engaged in various degrees of the task of materializing the archetypal ideas of the Logos. Although the work of bringing through the first realization of a new ideal has perforce to be in the hands of the dedicated psychic, all who are prepared to hear and to aspire can co-operate in the task of working out those ideals on the plane of matter. In fact the psychic, being by the very nature of his function, set apart and withdrawn from the workaday world of men, is not able to complete the task which he sets going, but has in his turn to hand on the torch to others. The pupils of the Masters, therefore, gather about themselves those to whom they teach the theory of esoteric science and imbue with its ideals, and it is these, not yet equipped with psychic faculties, not yet called to come apart and be separate, who serve their apprenticeship by carrying out the Logoidal ideals in the daily work among their fellow men in the ordinary walks of life. All pupils of the Masters, without exception, are recruited from among those who have thus served and been found faithful over few things.

Another branch of occult work is carried on by those who undertake no mundane tasks at all, but live apart and in seclusion, occupied solely with mental work. They perform the same function for the race as the Contemplative Orders perform for the Roman Church; they are a mighty

though invisible source of energy. Their work is entirely racial, and is
not for the helping of individuals in their personal problems. It is the
activity of these mental workers, visualizing ideals and neutralizing
spiritual evils, which steadies the nations. It cannot be too clearly realized,
however, that the political work of the true initiate is mental, and incursions
into political intrigue are to be deplored. The only exceptions to this
rule will be noted in the next section.

Herein we find that curious and exceedingly interesting section of occult
workers which are known as the occult police. They might equally well
be known as astral ambulance workers, for their task is twofold; those
cases which require their intervention for the safeguarding of society
usually also result in psychic casualties on both sides. Their task it is
to combat black occultism and deal occultly with those evils which arise
from the abuse of esoteric knowledge. This organization is highly
developed and ramifies in the most extraordinary network through our
social life. It does not meddle with normal crime, nor even political crime
or movements which a generation considers subversive but which a
later generation may look upon as the dawn of a new age; it concerns
itself solely with those movements which are availing themselves of the
little-known powers of the mind, and it deals with the mental element
on its own plane.

The occult police is unorganized on the physical plane save for small
fraternities whose members work in co-operation, but it acknowledges
the spiritual authority of Those who are concerned with the direction
of human evolution. It is on the side of liberal movements generally, but
also on that of law and order, knowing that it is essential that the
organization of civilization should not break down in the attempt to effect
reform, the remedy for the disease thus killing the patient.

In addition to protecting the race from organized attempts at subversion
of its racial ideals on the part of other races, it also guards it from the
insidious moral poison disseminated by occultists of the Left-hand Path,
whose activities are invariably bound up with either drug-taking or sexual
abnormalities. There is a psychic organization on the astral plane whereby
the Great White Brotherhood keeps track of the activities of these
individuals and brings them to the notice of those on the mundane plane
who are in a position to cope with them.

And so the work of the world gets done. There is always this invisible
counterpoise of dedicated mental workers throwing its weight as needed
to retain the balance of things. Putting aside the prizes that attract humanity,
utterly selfless, highly trained, taking great risks, these invisible workers
come and go about the world, known only to their brethren. Moved

like pieces upon the chessboard by Those upon the Inner Planes whom they serve, there is no apparent organization or cohesion among them upon the mundane plane; it is only the long series of opportune coincidences that attend their operations which point to something more than a fortuitous sequence of chances.

They are men and women, with no outward appearance of celebrity, who seek to avoid rather than to attract attention. All the deeper occult work is done in concealment, none knowing the whereabouts of the ritual lodges, firstly, in order to prevent any occult attack from being focussed upon them, and, secondly, in order that the members of the organization may not become known to any save their brethren, for the ramifications of the occult Orders are widespread and extend in some unexpected quarters.

The training received by the neophyte in these organizations, though it varies in detail, is similar in principles. Firstly, he is given a training in the metaphysics of occult science. He is taught to interpret the astral symbols so that he may realize their mental significance. The initiate of a true occult school does not make the mistake of turning a symbolic system of metaphysics into a geography and zoology of the astral plane. He knows that the marble Halls of Learning are but thought-forms used to focus power; he knowns that the King of the World and His myrmidons are organized systems of forces, not entities. He knows that the key to occulstism is psychology, and he leaves these superstitions to those who are without the gate of the Mystery Tradition.

He is instructed to live an abstemious and simple life, but not an eccentric one, and he is counselled not to diverge in his habits so far from the customs of his race as to break his connection with the group-mind. He is distinguished from the unenlightened, not by his clothes and personal habits, but by his mentality. Two qualities characterize him, his serenity and his courage; these are the *sine qua non* of an initiate. His training is designed to make of him a man of steel with a heart of compassion. He is tried in the furnace of sorrow and suffering until his nature undergoes the flux of the soul and can be remade. Then he is forged on the anvil of discipline by the hammer of danger. Out of that forging he comes as a steel blade. That blade may be a lancet, or it may be a sword, but nevertheless it is a blade. those who are 'interested in occultism' but little realize what goes to the tempering of the soul of an adept.

The mystic may till the garden of contemplation, but there is much more of the soldier than of the husbandman about the occultist. But, like the soldier, being under discipline, his is without responsibilities, and consequently he has in him something of the joyous and care-free nature of the soldier on leave. His wants are simple, and he knows that Those who command his service will see to it that they are supplied. The child in him remains unrepressed, and when he relaxes the bent bow of his psychism, he reverts to the child. This is very characteristic of the true adept, and distinguishes him from the charlatan who is for ever playing to the gallery.

The fully initiated adept should have the three-fold contacts of mystic devotion, occult wisdom, and the primitive nature-forces. The spiritual, the intellectual and the elemental must be perfectly balanced in his nature, and so disciplined by the will that they are absolutely flexible to the control of the judgment. The character of the adept may be summed up in one brief phase—he is a soldier-scholar dedicated to the service of God.

PART TWO
PRACTICAL OCCULTISM IN DAILY LIFE

1.

Practical Occultism in Daily Life I

A large number of letters pass through the office of the Society of the Inner Light, and a considerable proportion of these letters ask for help and advice concerning the application of occult forces and methods to the problems of everyday life. Obsessions, hauntings, occult attacks are comparatively rare and, as often as not, when investigated, turn out to be insane delusions. But persistent runs of bad luck; ill health which does not yield to ordinary methods of treatment, and concerning which doctors either disagree or declare they can find nothing the matter; disturbances due to unsound methods of psychic development, and evil influences in houses and places—these form a constant feature of our correspondence. We are also frequently asked concerning the interpretation of dream and vision symbols and the recovery of memories of past incarnations.

According to orthodox occult tradition the Mystery teaching should be strictly reserved for those who have offered their unreserved dedication and have had years of training and passed exacting tests. In other words, occultism meant adepthood or nothing. But with the general spread of occult knowledge which is taking place at the present time, a change is coming over the spirit of the movement. Just as community singing has taught everyone to enjoy taking part in the rendering of music, so the wayfaring man is asking that he shall be enabled to apply the methods of which he reads to the problems of his daily life. One cannot deny that this is a very reasonable request.

It is a difficult problem, however, to know how far the metaphysical and meta-psychic theories and methods of occultism can be made available for the untrained person, who is very apt to get hold of things by the wrong end and so enmesh himself still worse in his difficulties.

A special attitude and viewpoint is necessary for the satisfactory operation of occult forces; the man who would use them must be free from emotional bias and entirely detached and serene in his attitude, otherwise he makes confusion worse confounded. A knowledge of technicalities is not enough for occult work; it is the attitude that is all-important and that determines the nature of the ultimate issue. This attitude can only be arrived at by self-discipline and purification of character.

It is possible, however, to explain quite simply and practically what the requirements are; to teach the occult doctrines in their entirety, as this Society has long been doing is not possible, but it is possible to explain enough of methods of a suitable type to enable any reasonably intelligent and well-balanced person to make practical use of them in the everyday problems of life, even if its major ills must still be left to the expert.

The greater ceremonial methods are, of course, unsuitable for the use of anyone save a trained initiate; but there are many minor rites that can be used by anyone who can achieve a steady concentration. Moreover, an understanding of the occult principles applying to everyday life is invaluable as a prophylactic, enabling us to save ourselves from all manner of troubles. It also shows us the best way in which to approach and handle our problems, for there is a strategic approach to every problem—the flanking attack that out-manoeuvres, instead of the frontal attack of blind force. There are also tides in the affairs of men, and we may just as well time our operations so that we have these tides with us instead of against us. All these things are practical applications of occultism to everyday life, a knowledge of which must be of benefit.

So far as is possible, then, I propose to teach these things, and to teach them, not as rule-of-thumb methods, but with explanations of the occult principles on which they rest, so that those who try to use them may use them intelligently. How far they succeed depends upon the judgment they use in discerning the nature of the problems with which they are confronted. Diagnosis must always precede treatment, and the diagnosis of subtle psychic conditions is by no means a simple matter, because the subconscious element has to be recognized and allowed for, and it is not easy to be sufficiently impersonal and unbiased to achieve this when our problems are pressing acutely. However, we can but do the best we know, and we can often succeed in being more honest with ourselves than we are when we are trying to justify our position in the eyes of another.

Success also depends on our power to concentrate, holding the mind steady on a single idea. This, however, is almost entirely a matter of practice, and the regular use of certain exercises usually develops the required capacity fairly quickly.

Given these two things—a right judgment as to the nature of the problem and ability to concentrate, a great deal can be done, even by the uninitiated and untrained. Some problems can be worked out in their entirety and all problems can be made easier to bear, even if they remain unsolved.

It must not be thought, however, that I am going to teach how to blow the trumpets of Jericho. Some problems, of course, clear up readily when the underlying psychic cause is dealt with; others require steady and long-continued work for their solving. In others again, a mistaken diagnosis renders the world abortive. The experienced occultist, dealing with matters on the spot, ought to be able to make his diagnosis and forecast the outlook with a high degree of accuracy; but I am not writing for experienced occultists, but for those who are spelling out the letters of the occult alphabet; and although I am always glad to advise, as far as lies in my power, on such matters, it is seldom possible for me to be on the spot. The reader of these pages, therefore, will have to learn his lessons with the help of experience, which is an expensive school, but a very efficient one.

Basic Principles

There are many old-fashioned books, and some newer ones, too, which call themselves 'Home Doctors' or some such name. They tabulate a list in symptoms such as Stomach; pain in; sensation of fullness in, etc., and give a reference to the page where the appropriate remedy is listed, usually in doses suitable for navvies and blacksmiths. These are singularly unsatisfactory compilations, and probably send up the death-rate considerably by virtue of delayed operations and unrecognized cancer.

I do not propose to make that mistake in these pages, but to ask of the reader sufficient effort and attention to grasp certain basic principles in order that he may first and foremost arrive at a diagnosis and apply the occult methods intelligently.

First of all, we have to realize that the material plane, as we see it, is the end-result of a long chain of evolutionary processes that have gone on in the subtler planes, the realms of spirit, mind and astral ether. Consequently, every problem that we meet with on the physical plane will have a kind of soul, as it were, composed of factors from each of these levels of manifestation. It is important for us to realize this, because every problem is composite, and we have to determine the relative proportion of these different factors and discern upon which level the trouble has its root or nucleus. It is no use trying to deal with a problem by a simple astral exorcism if its root lies in some spiritual factor deep hidden in the soul.

We must always remember, however, that each plane has its own laws and conditions, and that these cannot be overridden by any power, however great, but only directed and used. But because each plane is ensouled and directed by the plane above, the extent to which its forces and mechanisms can be modified and directed is very great—much greater than is generally suspected. Nevertheless, there are well-defined limits to this power, and these must be accepted. It is in this respect that spiritual healing so often comes to grief, for it seldom admits limitations to what it is pleased to call the power of God, but which in all too many cases means the desire of the sufferer to be relieved from discomfort.

We must next realize that there are many forces, and many forms of existence, which do not extend down the planes as far as the physical; they may possess, for instance, a spiritual and mental, or spiritual, mental, and astro-etheric aspect, but no physical form. If we know how, we can in many cases extend these forces down the planes, and give them expression on the physical plane. This does not mean, however, that we are going to effect miracles and materializations, for in the great majority of cases the chosen vehicle of manifestation is the mind of the operator, and the operation therefore appears to take place by a concurrence of lucky chances in the way of nature. It is the power systematically, in chosen cases, to command these 'lucky chances', which shows that definite operations are being performed.

It must be noted, however, that discrimination has to be used in choosing suitable cases for these methods; they cannot be used as a routine operation for all who are uncomfortable in mind, body, or estate, and desire alterations.

It is the cases wherein these subtle forces are the predominant facts that are suitable for occult operations, and yield to them in a remarkably dramatic manner. but in all cases, however apparently materialistic, these subtle forces play a part, and they can be used to alleviate, if not to cure. A man crushed in a railway accident, for instance, or in the grip of an acute infection such as pneumonia, appears to have all his problems on the physical plane; yet this is far from being the case, for surgical shock and resistance to infection play a very important part in the issue, and these things belong to the subtler planes, for they depend upon vitality and temperament.

We must also remember that in order to assess with accuracy the nature of many types of problem, especially those relating to runs of bad luck and psychic pathologies, we must take into account the karma, or influences of previous incarnations. There are certain methods of assessing these, which we will describe in due course. Moreover, individual karma, or destiny, has to be worked out under the influence of the larger cycle of racial karma, which modifies or reinforces it, and this must also be taken into account.

To sum up, then, every problem is fourfold, spiritual, mental, astro-etheric, and physical. Each of these planes has its own laws, which cannot be abrogated, but can be directed. The causation of most problems also extends backwards in time to previous incarnations, and they are modfied in their working out by the prevailing influences of racial karma. It is in relation to all these factors, and not just one of them, that we have to work out our problems, and the proportions in which they are present vary in every problem.

2.

Practical Occultism in
Daily Life II

There are faculties in the soul of man which correspond to the subtler planes of existence, which exert an influence on these planes, and are in turn influenced by them. Most people ignore the existence of these planes and these faculties; yet if we observe life as it goes past us, we cannot fail to be struck by the fact that there are tides and eddies in the affairs of men which cannot be explained by the material sequence of cause and effect. It is these subtle tides and eddies that the occultist studies, and he has been able as a result of his studies to formulate certain definite laws with regard to them; these laws have a very immediate application to daily life and its problems.

These different planes do not lie one above another like the strata of rocks; they are different modes of existence, and can, any and all of them, occupy the same space at the same time, as sound, light, and warmth may do. The different aspects of consciousness are built up out of these different modes of existence just as the calcium which forms our bones is drawn from the mineral kingdom of the earth, and the water in our tissues is derived from the springs and rivers.

The calcium in our bones is in no way different from the calcium to be found in the tissues of plants or in the rocks of the earth's surface. Calcium behaves in the same way, and obeys the same laws wherever it is found; and so does water. Our heart is a pump just like any other pump, and the water in our blood behaves no differently to the water in the hot-water pipes. Precisely the same conditions prevail in the sphere of consciousness. The spark of Divine Spirit, which is the innermost core and nucleus of every human soul, is part of the Kingdom of Heaven. Our mental powers with their forces and images are part of the kingdom of mind; our emotional and instinctive nature is part of what occultists call the astral kingdom; and our body in its subtle etheric and dense physical aspect forms part of the kingdom of earth,. though be it remembered that earth has a subtle electro-magnetic aspect as well as a dense one.

Our body receives impressions from the physical plane through the five physical senses. It cannot perceive thought, or emotion, or the things of the spirit, save in so far as they are signalled to it by the effect they have on someone's body. But there are subtle senses, rudimentary in most people, more highly developed in some, which correspond to the three subtle levels of existence.

Most of us know instinctively the emotional state of anyone with whom we are in close touch; we know whether he is displeased, depressed, or frightened, even though he show no outward sign of his condition and may do his best to conceal it. The horse knows when the rider is afraid; the newborn child knows the difference between the nurse who will control it effectually and the mother who will give in to it, and behaves accordingly.

To explain these things as the subconscious interpretation of subtleties of gesture and expression makes demands on our credulity which are quite unnecessary. A far simpler and more comprehensive hypothesis explains that these things are due to the direct perception of emotional states by the corresponding factor in our consciousess, which reacts to them. Observe how the depressed person depresses his companions; how the angry one irritates them; how the timid one invites aggression.

We are influenced far more than we realize by the mental states of those about us; it is for this reason that a good morale is all-important in any organization. The bad employer does not realize this, and thinks that sullen and resentful workpeople can give him just as good value for the wages he pays as loyal and cheerful ones. One person in a workshop with a sense of injury will demoralize all the rest of the employees, even if he, for reasons of his own, gives no open expression to his grievance. If we observe business houses we shall see how the mental attitude of the person at the head goes right down through the whole staff, including those who have no personal contact with him. The inharmonious person works up resistances all round him which make life very heavy going for him. A kindly, genial, and even-tempered attitude is an effectual lubricant which by reducing friction increases power.

Does it follow from this that we are to yield ourselves without effort to the influences of whatever atmosphere we may find ourselves in? We are unwise if we do. Even if the atmosphere is congenial, it is not well to become too dependent on it lest we make ourselves so sensitive that we succumb to the least roughness when we have to face the outside world. If the atmosphere is uncongenial we need definite mental armour to protect us from its influences. Some teachers would say that we ought to set to work and reform the whole condition by means of thought power. Many novels have been written, and plays too, such as *The Passing of the Third Floor Back*, in support of this thesis, but this is an ambitious goal to set before ourselves at the start, and we may be wiser to content ourselves with the control of the inner kingdom to begin with. In any case, we cannot exercise much influence on our environment until it has ceased to have influence over us.

But while we need to recognize the very potent effect that a mental atmosphere can have upon us, let us remember that atmospheres are things which are made by human minds, and that we need not, and should not, yield ourselves inert and unresisting to their influence, but can do something towards the making of atmospheres on our own account. If we find ourselves in an atmosphere of disruption and discontent, we can set to work and make a centre of serenity and steadfastness in our own immediate neighbourhood. This we do by working from within outward, and by controlling our own reactions to the inharmonious environment.

As soon as the mental atmosphere ceases to be able to affect us, we are beginning to affect it. The stabilized inner atmosphere overflows, and the circle of harmony spreads like the ripples in a pool. Soon the more sensitive among our neighbours begin to feel the new influence that has been introduced into the mental atmosphere; they react to it in their turn and the influence is reinforced.

If, however, we had set to work in the first place to alter conditions which caused us unhappiness in order to recover our peace of mind, we should have failed to attain our end; for however much we might make and remake the world nearer to our heart's desire, there would still be the crumpled rose-leaf such as disturbed the princess in the fairy tale. But if we obtain dominion over the Inner Kingdom and are able to hold it steady in the face of external influences, so that we can say with St Paul, 'None of these things move me, . . .' we have become a factor to be reckoned with in the mental atmosphere; ceasing to be influenced, we become an influence.

There is an old story of two travellers who found the road rough to their feet. One said, 'Let us kill all the cattle in the world, and tan their hides, and make a carpet to cover the road from end to end so that we may walk in comfort.' But the other said, 'That is not possible, for the road is longer than the skins of all the cows in the country. Let us out of a single hide make shoes for our feet, and then our smooth carpet will go with us wherever we tread.'

The man who wants to alter his environment until he is happy is like the traveller who wanted to carpet the entire road; but the man who has gained control of his own reactions and rules his Inner Kingdom is like the man who has made shoes to protect his feet from the roughness of the path.

We must realize two things, then, if we are to avail ourselves of the Ancient Wisdom. Firstly, mental and emotional conditions have power to affect us without overt physical action; secondly, we must not allow reactions to these influences to gallop about like wild horses, but must break them in to harness. To perceive an influence is not necessarily to react to it. There is such a thing as counteracting it, and it is this which occult knowledge can teach us to do.

3.

The Control of Environment

As we saw in the previous chapter, the control of environment must begin with self-control, and until we cease to be influenced by surrounding conditions we cannot hope to exercise any mental influence over them. Paradoxically, it is only when our environment ceases to matter to us that we have the power to change it by mental means.

Having reached the point when we can obtain inner harmony, even if it be only for brief periods, we are in a position to undertake practical mental work; let us then consider how to set about this all-important task. Meditation should always precede any action or decision, and the meditation should be, curiously enough, not upon the subject of the problem that is to be solved, but rather upon spiritual development and unfoldment; upon selfless dedication to the highest ideal that can be conceived, and upon a clear and concrete formulation of that ideal itself. Then we should rise still higher in our aspiration, and meditate upon the limitless outpouring of spiritual life from which our individual lives take their rise, and should say over and over to ourselves as a mantram or litany the words, 'Limitless power. Absolute harmony. Eternal duration,' imaging the Absolute as white radiance pouring down upon us and our environment as we do so. We should live our lives and do our work to the accompaniment of this refrain for days together, until we find that it is beginning to take hold of us and repeat itself as a tune does that runs in one's head.

When this occurs and we find that the mantram is repeating itself automatically, we know that it has gone down into the subconscious mind and is reappearing on the surface again. Now we are in a position to do practical mental work because we have made subconscious contact with the Infinite, and even before any mental work is planned or done we shall be conscious of an inner change, a sense of wider life, of power, and freedom. The effect of these rhythmic repetitions of significant phrases is very great, as Coué showed in his system of auto-suggestion and as the Catholic Church has always known and taught in the repetition of prayers upon the beads of the rosary.

As soon as this inner change begins to make itself felt we are in a position to deal magically with our enviroment, but not before. It is not necessary that we should have achieved a condition of permanent equilibrium, for we can hardly expect this as long as we are in incarnation; but it does mean that we shall have moments of exaltation when we have risen above our environment and can say with St Paul— 'None of these things move me.'

Diagnosis, however, must always precede treatment; and before we can decide what remedy is needed we must classify the conditions with which we have to deal. This classification should always begin with our own subjective conditions, and we should ask ourselves what weaknesses in our nature have laid us open to the conditions of which we complain; and we shall find that lack of judgment, lack of endurance, lack of courage, lack of foresight, lack of energy, and many more of the little foxes that spoil the vines have been at the bottom of the trouble. Looking back over our lives we shall see many things that we should have done otherwise if we had been wiser and stronger. At this stage of the process we must never allow ourselves to lay the responsibility at the door of any other person or circumstance. If we have been wrongly dealt with by some person, we should not hold that person responsible and ourselves blameless, but should condemn ourselves for having been foolish enough to trust them, or having lacked the courage to resist them.

Having diagnosed our own weaknesses, our next task is to meditate upon the compensating qualities of those weaknesses. It is easy enough to find the opposite of the moral qualities that shall compensate any defect or overplus, but many people wonder how they can compensate for lack of wisdom or discernment. We shall find, however, that if we meditate upon humility, upon honesty with ourselves, and the courageous facing of unpleasant facts, that wisdom and discernment will not be far to seek in the practical affairs of life.

Our next task is to bring ourselves to accept the conditions in which we find ourselves as the result of our karma, and to stop resenting them and feeling sorry for ourselves; for these conditions are the very things we need to teach us the lessons of spiritual development; therefore we should accept them as just, and seek to learn what they have to teach us in the way of experience and spiritual development. This is an all-important step, and once we have achieved it and killed self-pity and resentment against fate, we have broken the karmic bonds that bind us to our conditions, and are in a position to work off the karma by means of conscious mental action, as the adepts do. But we can never hope to escape from a condition until we have broken by means of realization the karmic bond that binds us to that condition and fulfilled its lessons. That is why talismans made by any person except the one who uses them are valueless, and why the operations of ceremonial magic directed to mundane ends are apt to induce drastic reactions. The initiated adept, when he uses magical methods, diagnoses the karmic condition first and works accordingly; but the dabbler in occultism, and especially the unfortunate who purchases talismans and suchlike from the occult wholesalers who advertise their wares, is patching at effects and leaving causes untouched; and the cause is often at a spot remote from the effect, and sometimes responds in an unexpected manner when ignorantly tampered with. Anyone, however, who tries to work out his problems by reducing them to terms of spiritual first principles is on the right track, and has come into line with those forces which occultists call the Lords of Karma, so that these co-operate with him; and when this happens, problems clear up in a very surprising fashion.

Each of the operations described above will take several days to do; they are not things which are accomplished one after another at a single sitting. Each should be persevered with until an inner change and response is felt, and then, and then only, should the next phase be embarked upon.

Having made our peace, as it were, with the Lords of Karma, we are now in a position to turn from within outwards and contemplate our environment. When we do this we shall see that there are certain conditions which, unless we can alter them magically, must be accepted, for what cannot be cured must be endured; and also certain other conditions which, by the exercise of courage, determination, and energy, are capable of modification.

Let us consider first those conditions which we must accept as inevitable save as they are capable of magical alteration; and leaving all magical considerations for the present, make up our minds to achieve such a degree of self-control and mind training that we are able completely to prevent any emotional reaction to them, for this is the essential preliminary to magical control. We must rise above irritation by meditation on compassion and serenity; above fear and nervousness by learning to control our imagination, for fear is entirely the product of the imagination—we do not feel fear of the thing from which we are actually suffering in the immediate present—and when we remember how much we have suffered from our fears of things that never happened, and how our severest suffering has often come from things we did not anticipate, and of which therefore we felt no fear, we shall see that, although fear has its importance as a warning mechanism, it can readily overreach itself and be nothing but an intolerable nuisance, like any other bad habit, and as such is to be overcome. We should therefore train the imagination not to dwell upon things we fear, but rather to picture a happy issue out of all our afflictions and ourselves as sailing triumphantly into the port of our desires. This happy day-dreaming plays a far more important part in the lives of successful men and women than is generally realized. It is safe to say that no one who habitually indulges in timid and gloomy imaginings has ever achieved an ambitious goal. The person who habitually indulges in happy day-dreams develops a peculiar mental atmosphere which is best described by the word glamorous, and the more sensitive of the persons with whom he comes in contact are influenced by it and see him, not as he actually is, but as he pictures himself in his day-dreams. It is thus that wild-cat financiers raise money for their risky ventures, and crazy prophets collect disciples, and quack healers obtain the confidence of patients. There is a glamour about these visionaries which infects those with whom they come in contact; and as the belief of those about us induces self-confidence as surely as their distrust chills us, a circuit of action and reaction is set up which, like what is popularly called a vicious circle, increases in strength as it proceeds. It is a true saying that nothing succeeds like success.

What modern psychology calls the language of unconscious gesture is an extraordinarily eloquent thing, and is interpreted by the subconscious minds of others and reacted to in a way that neither they nor we realize in the very least. When our subconscious gestures announce that we expect a welcome, that we expect unquestioning acquiescence, nine people out of ten will respond and give us what we subconsciously signal that we are expecting. If our self-doubtings cause us to signal our diffidence, we are simply 'asking for trouble.' If, on the other hand, our habitual day-dreams have been concerned with our triumphant successes, we hang out unconscious banners of triumph, and nine out of ten persons will line up and march behind them unless our lack of wisdom is such that we have chosen an impossible line of country. The mongrel that crawls up cringing is asking for the boot, but the boot is applied with discretion to the upstanding Alsatian.

4.

Remembering Past Incarnations I

No sooner do people learn of the principles of reincarnation than they, not unnaturally, want to trace out their own karmic record in the past. We must not dismiss this desire as mere idle curiosity or foolish vanity, though it may contain elements of both these factors in varying proportions; it is a very useful thing to have some idea of one's past incarnations, but if this knowledge is to yield its full value, it is necessary that it should be first-hand, not second-hand; in other words, the actual recovery of past incarnations is an experience of altogether different calibre to having them read by a clairvoyant, however accurate. It is not without its value to have the record checked by a reliable clairvoyant, but the smallest fragment that we recover for ourselves is of infinitely greater value to us than the most accurate and complete record read off from the reflecting ether by another.

All the sting is gone from death the moment that we have glimpsed some authentic record of our personal past, for we know then, from personal experience, the immortality of the soul and its independence of bodily existence. It is well worth while to wait patiently till our own hands can draw back the curtain rather than have recourse to the clairvoyance of another, and so miss this great experience.

In order to unveil the past with accuracy, and with security from self-delusion, it is necessary to understand the basic principle of the doctrine of reincarnation. The esotericist recognizes two aspects of man, the Higher Self and the Lower Self. The Higher Self is a single, unified whole, which builds up around the Divine Spark, which is the nucleus of each human manifestation. The Lower Self is not a unified whole, but an ever-changing series of partial manifestations of the Higher Self, projected down into the planes of form and clothed upon with matter. The Higher Self is often spoken of as the Individuality, and each Lower Self as the Personality.

The word Individuality has for its root-meaning 'that which cannot be divided', in other words, a unit. The word Personality is derived from the Latin *persona*, or mask. In ancient Greece the players in the sacred Mystery plays, which formed part of the Dionysiac Mysteries, always wore masks, which were conventional representations of the part they took. We can readily imagine the player, in the course of the play-cycle which formed part of the Mystery celebrations, assuming first one mask and then another as his parts changed with the play that was being performed. Thus do we conceive of the immortal soul in the Mysteries; we think of it as assuming first one personality, *persona*, or mask, after another as it plays its allotted part in the successive Mystery plays which form the changing cycle of spiritual experience.

At the end of each incarnation the form aspect of the *persona* disintegrates and returns as dust to dust according to its plane, for the ensouling life which built it up and which holds all together is withdrawn. First the body, then the etheric double, then the astral form, and finally the concrete mind, all go thus, dust to dust, back to the abyss of primordial matter whence they were wrought into living substance by the breath of life that ensouled them. Nothing remains of these, save the tracks in space which they wore by the habitual reactions of their nature. These are sometimes called the shadows on the Reflecting Ether.

It is not easy to understand an idea so foreign to our mundane experience, but if we think of the reflecting ether, or Akasha, which is the aura of the earth, as a sensitive plate upon which is photographed every reflection that has ever fallen upon it, and from which it is possible, by appropriate means, which will be considered later, to pick out and develop single impressions at will, we shall have a rough approximation to an understanding of the process. It is the reading of the Akashic Records that is done by clairvoyants when they look up the past for a client; but it is something quite different which we do for ourselves when we remember our own past incarnations, and it is this latter process which is of such value to us. It is much more likely to be these Akashic reflections which are dramatized by the subconscious mind of the medium than any actual return of the dead *in propria persona* when communication with the departed takes place. This is the weak spot in spiritualistic manifestations, and explains the trifling and fragmentary nature of so much that is communicated by the so-called spirits of the departed.

When we revive our own memories, however, a different process takes place, and this will best be understood if we carry our investigation of the processes of death a step farther.

As each of the four bodies of form disintegrates, its essential essence is absorbed by the immortal and eternal Higher Self or Individuality of the person. It is this absorption which, by withdrawing the higher principles, in fact causes the dissolution of the subtler form-bodies after the physical vehicle, their essential instrument of manifestation and means of experience, is rendered unfit for use, either by age, accident, or disease.

It will be seen from this that the actual form aspect of each incarnation is dissolved and done with after each incarnation, but that its essential essence, the ripe fruit of experience, is absorbed by the Higher Self. Thus does the Higher Self grow and evolve. It might aptly be said that the soul grazes in the fields of earth, and lies down to chew the cud beside the still waters of Heaven.

If follows, then, that the only thing that persists, incarnation after incarnation, is the spiritual principle, the ethical essence, extracted from the sum total of the experiences of each earth-life; the life itself and its memories going into the discard after it has, as it were been sucked dry by the soul, which requires of it only this spiritual essence for its nutriment.

Let us now study the way in which memory is evoked. We can learn a great deal about this by observing what happens when we try to recite a poem of which we have not got too distinct a recollection. We know how hopeless it is to make a start unless someone can prompt us to the first line. Once we have that, off we go gaily, the poem unwinding itself spontaneously out of our subconscious memory until the thread of association breaks and we are once more in need of the indispensable help of the prompter if we are to start off afresh.

Stored in the Akasha, or Reflecting Ether, as previously described, are the memories of everything that has ever happened within the earth-sphere. If we can by any means secure the 'prompt' to any partiular set of memories, we can unwind them out of the aspect of subconsciousness in ourselves which corresponds to the Akasha. We have, of course, a natural link in connection with anything that happened in one of our own previous incarnations. We cannot however, pick this up on the planes of form, that is, of the concrete mind, by taking conscious thought, because there is no direct link between one incarnation and another on the planes of form; but we can pick it up via the Higher Self if we are able to think with the higher type of mentation, even if it be only for a brief flash.

In order to achieve this, we must consider our present life as a whole, and see if we can discern any recurring problem in it; for such a problem will probably be due to karmic causes. Consequently it will have its root in past incarnations, and we can use it as a guide-rope to cross the gulf fixed in the continuity of consciousness by each experience of death that we have undergone. It will thus be seen that we have followed this guide-rope up onto the level of the Higher Self by meditating upon the abstract essence of the experiences we have recognized to be karmic, that is, to be the immediate outcome of past lives. Our next problem is to follow our guide-rope down again onto the planes of form at a diverging angle from normal consciousness.

5.

Remembering Past Incarnations II

The translation of consciousness from one plane to another is best achieved by availing ourselves of the resources placed at our disposal by the simple and universal experience of sleep, when the normal concrete consciousness is in abeyance, the five physical senses are closed down, and subconsciousness, with all it contains, is left unguarded and undisciplined for a space.

After the light is extinguished, let us sink deeply into meditation on the spiritual essence that we have divined as being at the root of the particular set of karmic experiences we have selected for examination, but let us carefully refrain from dwelling upon these experiences in any shape or form; and let us equally carefully refrain from passing any moral judgment on them, or formulating any good resolutions arising out of them. We must simply think of these experiences as the food of the soul, and as teaching it certain lessons.

Let us continue like this, between sleeping and waking, making no effort of the will to keep ourselves awake, until fragments and flashes of pictures begin to rise in the imagination. These the orthodox scientist calls hypnogogics, and has little realization of their significance, nor of the uses to which they can be put. We should never strain after these pictures, nor make any conscious effort to formulate them. They must arise spontaneously if they are to be of any use to us. Let us remember that the skill in the use of this method lies in catching the impressions which are available to us as the mind crosses over from one state of consciousness to another and the two levels are momentarily blended. Then we are, in the words of astrology, on the cusp of consciousness and subconsciousness.

We must always bear in mind the fact that the impressions that have value are the spontaneous ones, because these alone well up from subconsciousness; the willed and directed ones are of the conscious mind, and these have no particular interest for us because we can command them at will. Consequently, let us have patience with ourselves, and remember that there is a knack to be acquired in the recovery of those impressions perceived when two opposite doors of the chambers of the mind happen to be open simultaneously. The trick lies in sliding easily and effortlessly from one state of consciousness to another with the mind's eyes open. It is a trick that has to be learnt, like the art of balancing on a bicycle, and we must be content to try many times, with the most fragmentary results before we can count upon getting anything worth having, though in some cases it may occasionally be that immediate results are obtained because the memories happen to be lying near the surface; but these are rare. When a definite reincarnation memory is obtained it is usually recognized by the emotion that surrounds it. We may see a perfect phantasmagoria of the past floating before the mind's eye as we lie between sleeping and waking in the darkness and silence, but it will have no special significance for us beyond that of a generalized beauty and interest. But when a fragment of one of our own authentic memories crops up, it will bring with it all its attendant emotional association, even if it be no more than a glimpse of the wall of a house where our physical tenement once dwelt. It is this uprush of emotion that tells us that we are on the right track.

The moment this occurs, we ought to rouse ourselves and concentrate on this fragment, so that we shall ensure that it shall not sink back again into subconsciousness and be lost to us. It is a good plan to have paper and pencil beside the bed, and to turn on the light and make notes or a rough sketch. In so doing we shall probably sacrifice a night's sleep, for these memories of the past are upheaving things when they reappear; but they need not necessarily be painful things: it may, in fact, be the fascination of them that drives sleep away for some hours.

Therefore, together with the writing materials to record the experience, we should also have the means of a light meal, such as biscuits and milk, in order that the gates may be closed again when the opening has been explored, for there is no formula so effective for closing the gates of consciousness as a little food in the stomach, especially hot food.

Next day we ought to try and ascertain to what period of history and to what country the fragment we have recaptured belongs, and then soak ourselves in the literature of that period and country. To this end historical novels are very useful, for they help us most effctually to see the past as a living human experience, and not as a dry-as-dust record in a museum. To this end we should also try to obtain illustrations of this epoch and place; and especially to see, and if possible handle, the actual relics of it such as may be found in museums. If we can by any fortunate chance possess ourselves of some authentic relic of this past, which shall act as a magnetic link, our experiment is greatly simplified, and whatever we obtain will come with much greater vividness.

The imagination will gradually build up a picture of this time and place, and if we are wise we shall limit ourselves strictly to one incarnation at a time; for we shall not only become confused, but form a very bad psychic habit, if we let the pictures of two or more incarnations run together and superimpose themselves one on another, like two exposures on one plate of a camera.

When the conscious mind has supplied itself with the necessary furniture and properties, we shall find that the fragments of memory are beginning to use these symbols and pictures in order to clothe themselves with flesh and dwell among us, as it were. In other words, the conscious mind is using these symbols and pictures to give form to the intangible impressions that are rising to the surface of the subconscious mind under the invocation of our interest and desire. We shall always know any genuine memory by the emotion it evokes.

Once a definite set of memories has begun to formulate itself into something coherent, we shall find comparatively little difficulty in applying the method to incarnation after incarnation; though we shall always find it easier to get the memories of incarnations when the body was of the same sex as the present one than to recall memories of incarnations when it was of the opposite sex. When we have gained proficiency in the method, however, it is a valuable experience to force the mind to recall memories of incarnations in a body of the opposite sex to that which we now occupy, for it gives a great expansion of consciousness and understanding, and is an experience never to be forgotten.

6.

Working Out Karma I

The word Karma is borrowed from the Eastern Tradition, but it is so widely used that it has become incorporated in the English language. The term used in the Western Tradition to describe the same influence is Destiny; but the Eastern word being more familiar, we will adhere to it in these pages.

Karma, or Destiny, is the influence of past lives as it affects our present life. It shows itself in two ways: in environment and in character. Our environmental karma determines the circumstances into which we shall be born and the congenital dispositions of the body with which we are born; for the body is just as much the environment of the soul as the home is the environment of the body. Temperament is not the same thing as character, for temperament is determined by the Ray-influence prevailing in the cosmic atmosphere at the time when the Divine Spark, which is the nucleus of the soul, began to be separated out from the formless mass of the Life-wave. Fundamental temperament is constant throughout the whole evolution of the Divine Spark, but character changes with every incarnation, and even in the course of an incarnation as experience works upon the personality. Character, in fact, may be defined as temperament modified by experience.

We come into incarnation, then, with a particular type of basic temperament which cannot be altered, but only developed and harmonized. In other words, we can be a good specimen or a poor specimen of our type, but one cannot make fish of flesh. The fundamental character of the personality in each incarnation is the result of the bias that the basic temperament has acquired in the course of its experiences in previous lives.

The greater part of karma works out by means of character, not by means of drastic happenings which are specially dealt to us out of the blue, as it were. If we observe the lives of others closely, we shall be able to trace this, though we may not see it so clearly in our own lives, which come too near our hearts for us to be able to see them in impartial perspective.

Allowing for the influence of the environment into which we are born and our congenital health, character exercises the predominant selective influence in determining the course of our lives. According to our character do we react to conditions; we choose when the choice is offered to us; we dominate or submit; direct or are driven. To either alternative of a pair of alternatives there hangs a long train of consequences. It will be seen, therefore, that the course of our lives is continually being biased in the same direction by our temperament and character.

Let me illustrate this by an example. A person may be of the dynamic, power-loving, ruling type; this is his basic temperament, determined by the Ray-influence that prevailed when his soul started off on its evolutionary journey. In this incarnation, however, there is a streak of laziness in him. In consequence of this he will be continually failing to grasp opportunity, either because he is disinclined to exert himself when opportunity comes along, or because he has failed to prepare himself to take advantage of it.

Such a man's life will be a tragic record of disappointments, capacities that never had their opportunity to display themselves, lack of recognition and appreciation.

His misfortunes may truly be said to be due to karmic causes, and these will undoubtedly show in the horoscope; but shall we say that it is circumstances which have dealt his karma to that man, or shall we say that it is his character that has dealt it to him?

The following test will show which it is. If he changes his character, a change in his karma will follow. If he becomes diligent instead of slothful, the next opportunity that comes along will not be missed, and so his luck will turn.

We do not appreciate the extent to which character deals out karma because it does it so subtly. It is the little foxes that get the opportunity to spoil the vines. Faults of character are not the only little foxes we have to reckon with; judgment plays an even more important part in determining the course of our fate; for it is possible to find a man with a very faulty character who has excellent judgment, and he will flourish like a green bay-tree.

Faulty judgment, however, rests at bottom on faults of character. There are errors of judgment which are due to impulsiveness, for we do not take sufficient trouble to ascertain the facts and think things out; other errors are due to our dislike of facing unpleasant facts, and so leaving them out of our calculations; vanity may lead us to over-estimate our own capacities and under-estimate the forces arrayed against us; lack of sympathy and imagination may cause us to fail to realize the kind of reaction we shall stir up in others by the things we do and the way we do them; laziness may lead to shirking, and get caught out; carelessness to lack of attention to detail; cruelty and unscrupulousness may array all sorts of resentments against us so that folk go out of their way to do us an ill turn; all these things are causes which we have set going with our own hands, but the results appear to come to us out of our environment; and yet they are simply due to the way in which our environment is reacting to us, which is a thing we generally leave out of our calculations when distributing the blame for the untoward occurrences that beset us.

A woman, for instance, complains, and not without reason, of her bad husband. But there must have been something unworthy in her to have been attracted by an unworthy mate. If people prefer pinchbeck gold to honest copper, they must not be surprised if the world breaks their false coin in half and throws the pieces back at them.

Let us accept as our basic fact that ninety per cent of karma comes to us by means of the reactions our environment makes to our way of dealing with it. When we set out to work off our karma, it is character wholly and solely that we work upon. If we can change our character, we can change our karma; for the selective bias will then alter its direction and environment will react to us differently.

The bias of a character is due to what is left over after the different influences in the last life have cancelled each other out in purgatory. Our good intention will weigh in the balance against our broken resolutions; our self-indulgences will detract from our capacities. Our struggles with our weaknesses will tell in the scales against the influence of those weaknesses, and these will have less power over us when we come into incarnation again. What is left over after this purgatorial process is completed gives us our bias in our next incarnation.

The aim of evolution is to develop perfect specimens of each type. We are not expected to change our type, but to harmonize it. One man may be the perfected administrator, another the perfected artist; another the perfected priest; but it is unwise to ask your artist to be an administrator: or your administrator to be a priest, for then we get princes of the Church who serve the Prince of this world.

Whatever is good in us is due to the basic temperament expressing itself in harmonized balance; whatever is bad is due to a bias of character. Our good karma is given us through our temperament, which is aligned to its own type of cosmic force; our evil karma comes to us through a tangle of forces setting up conflict when we are out of alignment with cosmic force. Therefore it is always unsatisfactory to allow anyone else to determine our ideals for us, for they are liable to drive square pegs into round holes. We have got to feel our way towards righteousness by means of wisdom. There is no quality which is a virtue in itself. We might as well say that because a teaspoonful of a certain medicine did us good, a teacupful will do us more good. This does not necessarily follow, as we can easily prove for ourselves.

Patience and meekness enhance the vices of the coward; courage and energy render more dangerous the vices of the bully. Even love can be misplaced and overdone and degenerate into emotional self-indulgence and silliness.

In view of all this, what can we do to work out our karma from the practical and immediate standpoint?

If our evil karma is due to a bias of character towards one side, it follows that if we can correct that bias, we shall correct that karma. A bias can be corrected, firstly, by steadily neutralizing it and building up the opposite qualities by means of meditation; and secondly, by altering our attitude towards life by the same means, and bringing ourselves into line with the cosmic forces of our Ray instead of getting athwart them and being swirled into eddy and backwash by contending forces.

7.

Working Out Karma II

We have seen the way in which karma determines character; and character, by determining the way in which we treat our environment, influences profoundly the way in which our environment treats us. In other words, our good and evil fortune depend to a very much greater extent than we realize upon the reactions our environment makes to our behaviour.

We have seen that it is possible to change our attitude towards life to a profound degree, and thereby to modify our karma. We come now to the root of the whole problem: the only approach to the working out of our karma. It may seem a hard saying to many, but the fact must be faced that karma is a thing to be accepted, not eluded.

This is the key to the whole problem. Karma must not only be accepted as inevitable, it must actually be welcomed as a scholarship in the school of life. When we have arrived at this attitude towards our karma its working out has begun. This does not mean, however, that it will set us no more problems, submit us to no more tests; we do not avoid karma by working it out; we come to the end of it by getting through it. We might just as well expect to be spared further lessons in arithmetic because we have got a sum right.

When an initiate sets out to work out his karma, he deliberately invokes it and speeds it up. The immediate result of this is twofold. Firstly, a crisis in his affairs; and secondly, a sudden access of power to deal with that crisis. After this critical period has been passed through, no more karma is left for him to work out, and he can truly say that all things work together for good for them that love God, for his good karma is now working unchecked; for the powers gained by him in the working-out remain, whereas the resistances have been overcome. He then experiences the curious opening-up of the way which is so often met with by those who make the unreserved dedication.

In dealing with our karma, therefore, we should make a virtue of necessity and accept it cheerfully, trying to see what lessons it has to teach us, what characteristics it is designed to develop in us, and actively and intelligently co-operate with the discipline of life in learning those lessons and developing those characteristics.

We should lift our eyes above the sea of troubles and gaze upon the ideal of perfected character. Let us imagine ourselves as we shall be when perfected by life after life of steadfast dedication—strong, wise, harmonized perfectly poised amid the ups and downs of life as a skilful rider controls a spirited horse, giving easily to its curvetings, yet directing and controlling it. With this ideal in mind, let us consider impersonally the difficulties that surround us and see how perfected wisdom, strength, and love would enable us to rise above them and work them out; then let us see how these very difficulties are developing in us the characteristics we need for our perfecting.

If we would look upon life as a school and try to understand its lessons how differently it would appear to us to what it does when we look upon it as an affliction—and how differently we should be able to deal with it!

It is open to anyone who can rise above a self-centred attitude to do what the initiate does, and invoke the Lords of Karma. Before he ventures upon this, however, he must have reached the point in spiritual development where he desires the good rather than the pleasant—the ideal of perfected character in preference to the pleasure-pain principl When his heart is really turned towards the ideal, the Dark Angel which according to Qabalistic tradition stands behind his left shoulder, become an initiator and shows him the Path.

In the language of the Mysteries, initiation by the Dark Angel follow upon the invocation of the Lords of Karma, and is the quickest and sure way to find the Path. Those who have taken this initiation come on the Path karma-free. According to Mystery tradition, the initiator alwa comes when called and asks us for the pass-word, and if we can gi that pass-word we are admitted to the Temple of the Mysteries. We not realize, however, that it.is life itself which is the Great Initiator, ar that the physical ceremony only ratifies the spiritual experience.

When we experience a whole-souled desire for the Way of Perfectio life always comes and asks us a test question. All those who have cor by the Path tell us that immediately upon the formulation of this des came a testing experience in the ordinary way of life. If they were ak to apply spiritual principles to the working out of this experience, th had answered the test question correctly, and passed within the Veil; thenceforward they see all life in terms of spiritual principle instead of physical sensation.

There is no mystery about the pass-word with which we must answer the Dark Angel of affliction, who comes to us in the name of the Lord— every great spiritual teacher who has come to mankind has told us what his pass-word is. It was uttered by Our Lord at the supreme testing in the Garden of Gethsemane—'Not my will, but Thine be done.' When we come to the point when we can say this in answer to the dark messenger of affliction that the Lords of Karma will send to question us when we invoke them, we shall hear the answering Word— 'Well done, good and faithful servant, enter ye into the joy of your Lord.'

It is the unreserved acceptance of our fate as the particular lesson we need for our spiritual development that is the key which unlocks the gate of our karmic bondage. When karma is accepted it is more than half overcome. We should make it our immediate aim to achieve serenity, and even happiness, under whatever circumstances the Lords of Karma may elect to send us. When they see that we have achieved serenity they will say, 'This lesson is learnt; it need not be repeated.' As long as any experience has power to disturb us, we have not mastered it, and will be repeated life after life until the lesson it has to teach is mastered.

The aim of karma is not to break us, but to make us. We need never fear that karma will be piled on karma until we are broken. It is never karma that breaks us; if we are broken it is because we have broken ourselves against it. Those who have seen wild ponies off the moors being broken to harness know something of the viewpoint of the Lords of Karma. As the fighting, stupid, vicious pony appears to the onlooking humans, so do we appear to the Lords of Karma.

The great majority of human beings are well-intentioned. The problem of the Lords of Karma is not so much to eradicate active evil as to get their pupils to understand what is required of them, for we are just as much a lower order of creation to them as the animals are to us. Let us look upon the buffetings of fate as the barkings, and if need be the shrewd nippings of the sheepdog, and the stick-wavings and shouts of the shepherd trying to induce us to enter the green pastures awaiting us, and cease to consider them as the blind thwartings of our legitimate desires by an unkind Fate.

When we utter those mightiest of all the Words of Power, 'Not my will, but Thine be done,' we come automatically into line with cosmic force, and this new will in us is no longer thwarted, but carried swiftly to its goal by the tides of the spiritual universe. This will, however, is the will to spiritual perfection; it does not gratify either our vanity or our greed; nor will it shelter our cowardice or sloth. The path by which it leads us will wind uphill all the way, but it will be sunlit and serene and we shall never lack shelter for the night.

8.

Divination: Its Uses and Limits

Divination is really a spiritual diagnosis whereby we try to discover what subtle influences are at work in our affairs. It can be exceedingly helpful if rightly done; but it can be exceedingly harmful if improperly done because of the depressing suggestion and sowing of unwarranted suspicion to which it can give rise.

A divination should be regarded as a weather-vane which shows which way the winds of the invisible forces are blowing; but it should always be remembered that a weather-vane is not meant to determine the course that a ship is to take; it merely indicates how best to trim the sails.

There are two types of divination, one of which is purely psychic, relying upon vision or communication from spirits, and employing at most a crystal or a pool of ink to aid vision. The other type makes use of a set of arbitrary symbols, such as playing cards, or the prick-figures of geomancy, and reads the significance of the chance dealing of these according to a definite code, thus considerably reducing, but by no means eliminating, the personal factor.

Anyone with practical experience of seership knows that to try to obtain enlightenment by psychic means concerning any matter in which one has a strong emotional bias is seldom satisfactory, for the bias vitiates the results to such a degree that they may prove most misleading. It is well known that no seer can skry for himself in any matter in which he himself is intimately concerned. This is even true when resort is had to another psychic; for the strong emotion in the mind of the querent is very apt to influence the psychic unconsciously, so that the results obtained may either be coloured by desire, or, if the influence is unconsciously resisted, may lean to the other extreme.

The best thing to do under such circumstances is to employ one of the methods of divination in which the symbols employed are shaken together and dealt out by chance. Of these the Tarot is far and away the best, because much the most subtle and comprehensive, and those who possess the higher understanding can obtain an insight into the spiritual factors in the case under investigation.

To use the Tarot properly, however, requires a very great deal of preparation, and the preparation does not consist merely in a knowledge of the significance of the cards, but in getting in touch with the forces behind the cards. An adequate rule-of-thumb use of it, however, can be made by any sincere person for himself, though it is doubtful if he could use it satisfactorily for anyone else.

Obtain a *new* pack of Tarot cards, for a used one will be too full of other people's magnetism to be reliable, and carry them on the person, and sleep with them under the pillow, and handle them and ponder upon the meaning of the pictures in the light of what the book of instructions has to say about them until the significance of each picture is realized. It does not matter greatly which pack is used, whether the quaint, hideous, archaic ones, or the very beautiful ones redrawn in recent times for Mr A. E. Waite; it is not the details of the cards that matter, but that they should serve as reminders, as it were, of the ideas underlying them. As soon as one perceives some sort of significance in the picture on a card, one has made a link with that card, and its appearance in the divination will mean something.

Having got in touch with one's chosen pack, the next thing is to lay out a divination according to whatever system is chosen, work it out according to the book, and note down the results obtained and the position in which the cards fell. Repeat the process a second time, and a third time, upon each occasion keeping accurate notes of the fall of the cards, and, of course, thoroughly shuffling the cards between each lay-out. If certain cards keep on coming up, and especially if they come up in approximately the same positions, or even if cards of the same type predominate through the three divinations, it may safely be concluded that the system is working satisfactorily, and a divination may be made on the basis of the recurring cards. But if the three divinations bear no resemblance to each other; if even the balance of the four suits does not remain constant for at least two out of the three, and if none of the Greater Trumps turn up more than once, then it must be concluded that the Tarot is not working for the diviner, and the divination should be abandoned. The same principles apply if divinations are done with ordinary playing-cards, though this method is not nearly so sensitive and comprehensive as Tarot divinations.

Divination is a thing that cannot be learnt out of books, but builds up gradually as a system of associated ideas in the mind of the operator. Moreover, one varies very much in one's capacity for divination; upon one occasion one may be absolutely inspired, the cards recur and recur, and one reads with the most extraordinary insight, one thing leading to another in an endless train; at another time, one may have to spell out the meaning of the lay-out with reference to the book for almost every card. It will always be found that it is useless to force a divination; if the interpretation does not leap spontaneously to the mind it is unlikely to contain much insight.

Far better results can be obtained in this way than by going to dubious professionals. The only person who can do better for one than one can do for oneself is an initiate who has specialized in the Tarot; these, however, will never do the work for a fee, and therefore it is only under special circumstances that one can obtain such a reading.

All visions and voices that are heard when one is under strain should be highly suspect, for even if they spoke the truth they would be unwholesome symptoms, indicating that the mind is tending to come apart, to dissociate, under the strain. Every experienced occultist always closes down all supernormal faculties when conditions are adverse, because he knows that the still small voice is never heard in the thunder or the whirlwind, but only in the silence. The higher contacts give a sense of power, of protection, of peace; they do not speak with voices. It can never be said too often that whenever the Unseen becomes visible to the physical eye, or audible to the physical ear, something is going wrong with the works, for the planes are leaking the one into the other and unless the leakage can be stopped, mental unbalance will result.

Even to see with the inner eye, and hear with the inner ear, realizing all the time that the impressions are subjective, needs caution; the greatest safeguard we can have in the use of any psychic powers we may possess is to understand the psychology of them, and keep constantly in mind the fact that what we are perceiving is not the thing itself, but a dream-like cartoon of it that is being dramatized by our subconscious minds.

The further we advance in our spiritual development, the less difference will there be between the operation of our higher consciousness and our normal mentality. Seership is an illuminated state of the normal mind in which discernment is raised to a very high degree. The more primitive and unevolved the nature, the more startling and abnormal the phenomena.

The problem of the horoscope is a very perplexing one. A horoscope can be a very great help; it can also be a most pernicious influence, full of poisonous suggestions. Everything depends upon the wisdom and spiritual quality of the astrologer. The right kind of astrologer can be as helpful as the right kind of priest. Let it be remembered, however, that the professional, advertising astrologer is obliged to do an enormous amount of hack-work and it is almost impossible for him to keep his spiritual virginity. Moreover, no well-known astrologer, with a large practice, can do personally all the horoscopes he receives; the work is farmed out. You are more likely to receive good value from a friend who is studying astrology for its own sake than from the professional who is grinding out horoscopes all day long for a living, and who may be at the third or fourth remove from the celebrity to whom you sent your guinea.

Professional occultism, which is a breach of the very basis of the spiritual sciences, is a sordid and unsatisfactory business, which blesses neither those who do it nor those who have it done. I have never seen anything but harm come from running round from one soothsayer to another; nor anyone who made a living out of it and kept their spiritual powers unimpaired.

9.

The Use and Abuse
of Mind Power

It is by no means simple to find a standard by which to judge the limits of the justifiable use of occult knowledge. There is a borderline of use and abuse of which common sense and common honesty must form the touchstone, but it may be possible to lay down certain rules to help in arriving at a judgment in individual cases. We can at least hope to find a middle way between the extremes indicated by the advertisements of certain transatlantic organizations upon the one hand, and the doctrine that an intiate may never make use of occult power for his own personal ends upon the other.

The more blatant of the get-what-you-want courses in spiritual development are of such a nature that even the advertisements find it difficult to justify them, and one marvels that a sufficient number of sufficiently silly persons can be found to make them pay.

One also marvels that the *ipse dixit* adepts can get people to believe them when they say that their omission to make use of their powers on their own behalf is due to the strictness of their principles. 'Physician, heal thyself', is a not unreasonable test to impose on our spiritual pastors and masters.

The notion that the more spiritual one is, the more poverty-striken one should be is derived from the East, as is much of our religious ethics; and because the temperament, physical conditions, and climate of India and Palestine, the chief sources of our spiritual inspiration, are entirely different from our own, some of the accepted precepts are by common consent given no more than lip-service because they prove impractical for men and women of Nordic race in a cold climate.

This is not a good thing for the spiritual morale of a race. If it is so generally agreed that certain commandments are so impractical that they can be ignored without incurring social odium, the whole basis of dogmatic morality becomes suspect, and its writ ceases to run outside the inner circle of ascetics. What we need is an ethical standard that shall do justice between man and man and spur the soul forward on its evolutionary path.

Let us realize first of all that there are two ways in which esoteric knowledge can be used in order to 'better ourselves' materially. It is possible to influence the minds and wills of our fellow men so that they shall give us what we want; it is also possible to draw directly from the great cosmic reservoirs of undifferentiated force. The former way is the way of Black Magic; the latter is the way of White Magic. An operation, then, passes the first test when it does no harm to any creature; for if it is axiomatic that we have no right to interfere with the free-will and responsibility of any soul, even for his own good, save in an emergency, how much less have we the right to try to influence anyone for our own good?

Jesus said, 'I am come that they might have life, and that they might have it more abundantly.' This should be the keynote of our operations to secure better material conditions by mental and spiritual means. We should seek the spiritual sources of life and drink therefrom. This we do by means of meditation performed upon the Great Unmanifest, the Source of all Being; realizing its infinity, omnipotence, and eternal duration. The source of our being is in this ever-outpouring, infinite energy; the amount of this energy we receive is limited solely by our capacity for realization; if we can increase our realization and get rid of our inhibitions, we correspondingly increase our intake of cosmic energy, and this energy is transmuted within our being into all the different forms of activity that go to make up human life.

If our vital energy goes up, every factor in our nature is quickened and intensified; the artist paints with new power and inspiration; the insight of the scientist is redoubled; the skill and strength of the manual worker are increased; the intelligence and happiness of a child—the beauty and charm of a woman—whatever we are becomes intensified. This, in fact, is the real basis of spiritual healing—the true spiritual healing as distinguished from healing by suggestion; the vis medicatrix naturae, which is the only real curative agent, becomes greatly increased, and, thus increased, can often ameliorate, and sometimes completely cure, conditions that previously resisted it.

We must realize, however, that the action of the inpouring cosmic force is not selective; every aspect of our nature is intensified by its influence; consequently, whatever is unregenerate comes up immediately in an acute form, and unless we can pass safely through the spiritual crisis that always ensues in some form or another when spiritual power is called down, our last state will be considerably worse than our first. The Christian Scientists, who have a wider experience than anyone else of mind-healing, call this crisis 'Chemicalization,' and always watch out for it in treating their patients and regard it as a sign that the treatment is proving effectual.

If we are working upon right lines, however, the crisis is minimized, for the true line of approach to the source of spiritual power is in the spirit of the words, 'Not my will, but Thine be done.' There are two methods of drawing down this power—the ceremonial one and the meditative one. The ceremonial one should only be used for concentrating the power that has already been contacted by meditative means; it is a method only suited to the advanced worker, who has been disciplined and purified; we need not therefore consider it in these pages, save to warn against its use, as in inexpert hands it can produce disastrous results. The meditative method consists in increasing awareness by means of contemplation of symbols of infinity, eternity, and omnipotence, affirming and reaffirming the perfect harmony of cosmic law, and picturing our own relationship to that which we are contemplating. With increasing realization there comes increasing vitality, mental capacity, and poise. Upon this basis of increased capacity and poise all else is built up. If what we need is more money, we will soon find we can earn more because our market value as human beings has gone up. If what we want is work, we shall find little difficulty in obtaining an engagement because everyone we come in contact with will sense unconsciously the vitality and serenity that animates us. If we have life-problems to work out, we shall find that increased serenity lessens our reactions to them, and when we cease to react, we cease to stir them up; our increasing vitality gives us more energy and courage with which to deal with them; our increased mental capacity gives us increased insight with which to solve them; and one thing leading to another, 'all things work together for good to them that love God.'

This is the only right and proper method of using occult power for our own purposes; and it would be difficult to see what ethical objection could be advanced against such use for legitimate ends; for not only does it defraud no man, but increases our spiritual stature and advances us upon the evolutionary path.

Our next problem is to consider what are legitimate ends. We may safely say that whatever brings harmony where there was disharmony leads to a legitimate end. This may sound a very simple and satisfactory solution of all our problems. We have merely to make up our minds what we want and go ahead and get it.

But it is not quite as simple as all that. What we may need to make us happy is not more money, or the love of some particular person, but an entire change of attitude towards life; for if our attitude to life is basically wrong we shall reverse the process of the Midas touch and turn everything we handle to dross.

The only safe thing to do when we want our problems straightened out is to surrender ourselves unreservedly to cosmic law and determine to do the right thing, whatever it costs. When we do this we come down to bedrock, and whatever is built then stands on a firm foundation; but however much cosmic power we call down, we cannot build an enduring dwelling on foundations of sand.

We must never consider expediency when we are working by means of cosmic force; let us learn to trust in its infinity and omnipotence, and rely upon being able to call down sufficient force to do whatever is needful to bring all things to a just and harmonious conclusion.

There is one point that recurs so often in the questions asked by students that it is well to deal with it specifically. How far is it justifiable to use this method for obtaining money? Here again a great deal must be left to a conscience enlightened by common sense.

We are very unwise to outline our askings when we approach the Source of All Life. Rather should we ask for harmony and increasing fullness of life, and leave it to Infinite Wisdom to discern our real needs; for needs and wants are not always the same thing. In nine cases out of ten a change of heart is needed as well as change of circumstances before harmony can come in; and in a goodly proportion of those cases a change of heart is all that is needed, and the circumstances will do well enough when we approach them properly.

We make a fundamental error when we try to obtain happiness by the possession of things. Seek first the Kingdom of Heaven which is within us, and all these things that make for happiness shall be added unto us through a thousand unexpected channels till they are more than we can ask or think.

But as it is obvious that money is the key to so much in this world, and that although the possession of it cannot give us happiness, the lack of it can make it exceedingly difficult for us to be happy, we must squarely face the problem as to how far we may expect fullness of life to express itself in the form of more abundant money. We know well what all the great religious teachers have had to say about money, and how scantily equipped they were with this world's goods; we also know that our Lord said that it was easier for a camel to pass through the eye of a needle than for a rich man to enter the Kingdom of Heaven. In the face of all this, are we right in regarding money as a legitimate need for which we may use spiritual forces without injuring ourselves spiritually?

The key to this problem lies, I think, in the realization that it is the simplicity of life which comes through a realization of what are the essentials and what are the inessentials that is the one thing needful; for the needs of this essential simplicity I believe we may justifiably invoke spiritual aid. This simplicity should include orderliness, seemliness and beauty, and the recreation that keeps the balance of our natures intact. It should also include scope for the development of our capacities. I cannot conceive, however, that it should include luxury or display, or enable us to put our neighbours in the shade.

If we value spiritual things, this will be our natural mode of living, for we shall not want to be distracted by the much care that goes with much cattle. If we have not got the roots of spiritual realization in us, we had better leave spiritual power alone, for the first thing it does when it visits us is to burn up the dross in our natures, and if the proportion of dross to pure gold is too high, the consequences may not be all we had hoped for. One must have the right kind of desires before one can safely trust spiritual forces for their fulfilment. In any case, we must always be prepared to offer a greater or lesser change of heart as our contribution to the task.

10.

Etheric Magnetism I

Our knowledge of electricity is of comparatively recent development; and although extensive practical applications have been made of this elusive energy, we are still ignorant concerning its real nature. Recent advances in knowledge, however, have shown us that its distribution is much wider-spread than had previously been recognized; in fact, we might safely say that electricity is all-pervasive, and it only requires the development of instruments of sufficient sensitiveness to demonstrate the fact.

It had long been known that the human body was of the nature of an electric battery; that nervous impulses were transmitted by means of weak electric currents running along the nerve fibres, and that the electrical conductivity of the body changed with the change of emotional states. Recent discovery has produced an instrument of such sensitiveness that not only can it demonstrate that the human body gives off electrical energy, but can actually measure the amount—greater and less in different individuals—finding it to be the greatest in young, virile males, and least in the elderly and those in weak health.

A wide range of experimental work opens up along these lines, and it will be interesting to see how closely it agrees with the traditions of esoteric science. For this electrical energy of the human body has long been known to initiates, although other names have been given to it than those that modern science is coining to fit the facts that are coming to light, and it is well known to be the basis of much occult phenomena.

Its practical applications in our daily lives are fairly widely realized; but unfortunately the value of this knowledge has been vitiated by the amount of supersitition and auto-suggestion that have grown up around it. We need to find the middle way between a stubborn disregard of all subtle influences that exposes us to much needless discomfort, or even more serious harm, and a hyper-suggestible faddiness that ends in hypochondriasis.

Because we recognize the actuality of an influence, it does not follow that we must forthwith surrender to it. There are two ways in which we should react to it: firstly, by learning all we can about it and making use of it medicinally, as it were, learning its indications and dosage, and how to direct and control its activities; and secondly, by learning how to neutralize or deflect it if its influences under certain conditions should be found deleterious.

Experimental science has now caught up with esoteric tradition in asserting that every living creature is an electric battery, and has learnt to measure the electrical energy quantitatively; the next step will be the demonstration of the varying qualitative nature of the electrical energy generated by that living battery. This diversity of quality esoteric science clearly recognizes, and classifies under the seven planetary influences, using various divinatory methods as tests and indicators. By these means a rough approximation can be arrived at, though we shall have to wait for experimental science to give us precise methods of testing and measuring.

Meanwhile, however, we can take the esoteric doctrines as working hypotheses and show their practical application to our lives; a very small amount of experimenting along these lines will soon convince us of the actuality of the influences we are dealing with.

First and foremost, let us conceive of every form, whether animate or inanimate, as emanating a magnetic field of electrical energy. Then let us conceive of the exchange of magnetism between any objects that come within range of each others' electrical fields. Let us also remember that this magnetism varies in quality as well as in quantity, and that the variation depends upon the nature of the rhythm of its pulsating energies. It will follow then, that we are all the time receiving electromagnetic influences of a very subtle nature from everything with which we come in contact, and from every person with whom we are in any sort of relationship. Equally it follows that all and each of these will be taking electrical energy from us according to their individual nature.

We must not, however, run away with the idea that all interchange of magnetic energies is of the nature of vampirism. This is far from being the case. To give and receive magnetism is normal to us, and the lack of such an interchange affects us as harmfully as the lack of the necessary vitamins.

There is a normal exchange of magnetism which is intensely stimulating, both to those who give and to those who receive; the breaking of this circuit produces distinct nervous pathologies which can only be cured by its restoration. This interchange can, however, be subject to certain pathologies, and these also we must consider in their place.

We can see both these aspects of magnetic influence clearly illustrated in the relationship between mother and child. A young child will not thrive without intimate personal love and contact with someone who cares for it as an individual. This is so well known that nowadays young children are never herded together in large orphanages, but farmed out in individual cottage homes in small groups; for it was found that the infant mortality in the mass rearing of babies was abnormally high, and the intelligence developing among them abnormally low.

So tangible is the influence of the magnetism of the mother that a well-known doctor recommends that a nervous, highly-strung mother should not hold her child in her arms, but support it on a cushion so as to insulate it from her disturbed magnetic influence.

The influence of the father is just as important as that of the mother, but it does not reach the child directly during its earliest years, but comes to it through the mother. This has only to be pointed out to be recognized, for how different is the influence transmitted to her child by a woman happy and secure in her marriage from that transmitted by one who is uneasy and unhappy.

As the child grows older, however, it should normally outgrow the influence of the mother-magnetism and become receptive to the influence of the father-magnetism, which ushers it into the group mind of the race and makes it a regular member thereof. For just as the mother gives birth to a child as a separate physical individual, so the father gives birth to it as a social individual. We do not give sufficient importance to the part played by the race-life in our individual lives, nor recognize that man is a social animal, and that his group relationships are as much a part of his mental being as his other instincts.

In this social relationship, both mundane and psychological, the father is all-important. It is a great mistake to leave the children to the management of the mother after the nursery days are over. They are far better off under the discipline of the more rough-and-ready male, who does not fuss and fidget over trifles and gives a sound thrashing for serious offences, than in the over-sensitive and over-sensitizing hands of the female parent. More freedom and less tenderness are a better preparation for a life than the 'mother-love' so often and so unwisely given. Mental specialists know well the results brought about by the over-prolonging of the sensitizing feminine magnetism and the consequent starvation of the invigorating male magnetism.

It is for this reason that the family and not the individual must always remain the prime social unit, and that the experiments in child-culture undertaken by the Soviet have had to be modified: it is for this reason also that free love is an impractical proposition because it produces homeless children, and a child never thrives outside a home. A home is as essential to a child as a nest to a bird. For in the home, and in the home alone, can he enjoy the right magnetic conditions for his development.

In the immediate magnetism of his mother's arms he receives essential spiritual vitamins during his earliest years. Later, in the atmosphere of his father's pride and protectiveness, he receives the influences essential for his development as a social being. Adequate substitutes are hard to find for these two personal relationships. The mother's is, perhaps, the easiest to replace, because most women get fond of any small child that is in their care. But the average man can seldom be got to feel any pride in someone else's offspring, and it is this family pride behind him which is such an invaluable support to an adolescent finding his place in the great world opening before him.

There is no substitute for the magnetism given off by happiness and affection, and pride and protection within a secure home circle, and children who have this start in life have an incalculable advantage over those who are born of contention. Moreover, they will tend to reproduce their own home conditions when they come to have a home and children of their own.

11.

Etheric Magnetism II

Etheric magnetism plays a very important part in the relationship between the sexes. We usually think of this relationship as being physical and emotional; we do not realize that it is also etheric, and that the etheric factor is an exceedingly important one, and explains many things which cannot be explained in any other way.

Those who observe men and women know that if a group of women, however large, be cut off entirely from all association with males, a very peculiar mental atmosphere grows up among them, and they deteriorate individually, developing all manner of neurotic traits. This degeneration does not take place in the case of men; in fact they tend periodically to seek seclusion from the society of women in order that they may, as it were, 'be themselves' without restraint. It is also noticeable that in a group of women, even though they include no married women, if they either work with, or have social relations with men, the peculiar atmosphere and neurotic condition does not develop. What is the reason for this?

The reason is that the female receives etheric magnetism from the male whenever there is any degree of sympathy between then, whether in the comradeship of the workshop or the social relationships of dancing and dining or playing games together. The amount of magnetism she receives is in proportion to the degree of sympathy, which ranges from simple kindliness and good will, through all degrees of flirtation and love-making up to the final consummation in physical union. Just as with vitamins, if this magnetism is completely lacking, deficiency diseases develop in course of time, but it only requires a very small proportion of this essential magnetism to maintain the soul in health. Enough can be picked up from even casual comradeships, provided there are plenty of them.

The male, for his part, is throwing off this magnetism all the time; therefore isolation from the companionship of women does not present a problem to him. On the other hand, if he is constantly in the company of women who are taking this magnetism from him, especially if he be the only male in a group of females, more magnetism tends to be drawn from him than he can comfortably spare, and his instinct is to seek comradeship in exclusively male society for a period, so that he has the use of his own magnetism for his own purposes, and can build up his personality without interference. The man who is constantly in the society of a group of women and lacks male companionship tends to lose his personality and be made negative; as witness the only son in a family of sisters where there is no father.

It has often been pointed out that there is a curious discrepancy in the relationship of the sexes, in that although the male has a definite physical need of the female, the female has no such need of the male. But this discrepancy is more apparent than real; for the female has just as definite an etheric need of the male as he has a physical need of her. It is this fact that holds incompatible couples together in the most surprising manner. One would think that their relationship would be a cause of nothing except mutual discomfort, and that they would be far happier apart; but as a matter of fact they have a curious need of each other, and are not content when separate.

This tie remains and binds, even when there has been legal divorce, until such time as both parties have formed fresh relationships. It is curious how much profound sex psychology was embodied in the old divorce law of England, which had grown up, like the rest of the common law, out of precedent and experience. That law declared that if adultery were condoned, that is to say, if the guilty party were received back into the marriage relationship again, there could be no divorce in respect of that offence. This is sound esoteric psychology; for the re-establishment of marriage relationship would renew the magnetic link broken by the adultery.

In a happy marriage, where there is both affection and natural physical relationship—and no marriage can be happy without these two factors—a body of magnetism gradually builds up which includes both personalities in a single aura. It is in this single, shared aura that the real significance of marriage lies, as distinguished from irregular relationships. It is noteworthy that when pension inquiries during the War revealed how great was the number of unlegalized unions that were functioning as marriages, it became necessary to adjust the pension regulations accordingly, and the woman who had been regularly living with a man as his wife was enabled to draw separation allowance and pension in the event of his death. These unlegalized unions held for better for worse with exactly the same qualities of endurance as those that were recognized by Church and State.

It is this double aura which really constitutes the home. A married couple can make their home in a single room, and it can still be a home; they can make it in a caravan that moves on every day; they cannot make it, however, where there is no continuity of abiding-place, for the magnetism includes the objects in daily use. This is indicated in the popular expression, 'Get a home together', which means obtain the needful furnishings for the carrying on of daily life.

Life inside this aura is entirely different to life outside it; for it has a peculiar power to inhibit outside influences. The person safe inside a well-established marriage aura is very resistive to suggestion coming from outside. This aura has a peculiar power to re-establish the poise of either partner when it has been shaken by the rubs of life; where there is mutual affection and respect, the self-esteem, shaken by the rude contacts of the world, is quickly restored. This is one of the most valuable things in marriage, for there is nothing more difficult than to handle affairs successfully when one's self-confidence is shaken.

This power of the home to resist outside interference is one of the last things to go when a marriage is breaking up. Anyone who has ever interfered between husband and wife does not need to be told this twice. They will stop any quarrel to unite against outside aggression.

When the marriage aura becomes well established the two are indeed made one, and each feels the other to be an extension of his or her self, so that any injury or deprecation to the one is felt as an injury to the other. Curiously enough, this applies even when there is ill will between the partners. Once the marriage aura has been established, it will stand a surprising amount of strain without giving way; it is this factor that complicates the divorce problem in a very curious manner. Unless there has been adultery, it is very difficult to dissolve a marriage aura. The act of adultery takes the guilty party right out of the marriage aura, and if he does not re-enter it by returning to eat and sleep under the family roof, he remains out, and the marriage ceases to function. Here again the common law speaks esoteric truth when it divorces 'from bed and board.' For it is a curious fact that to eat with a person establishes a psychic link. This is recognized in the customs of primitive peoples in relation to hospitality, especially among those who look upon hospitality as a sacred duty; the man with whom they have eaten is safe from attack for several hours after he leaves their camp, that is to say, until the food within him is digested. When a married couple reach the point when they take their meals separately, as well as occupy separate rooms, there is very little left of the marriage aura. The magnetism of the common meal is very potent; when a quarrel is made up, it is a common custom to have a drink together. When the point is reached where one person says to another, 'I will not eat with you,' the breach is unhealable. A very curious effect is produced by the person who refuses to share in a toast.

The evil effect of promiscuous relationships has its roots in the damage it does to the etheric magnetism of both parties. No marriage aura can build up; consequently the peculiar steadying and protective effects of marriage are lacking; irregular relationships are a stimulant, but not a food; they create appetite, and never wholly satisfy it. For the significance of sex lies only partly on the physical plane; and where the relationship is limited to the physical, certain essential spiritual vitamins are still lacking. A marriage aura is a thing that takes time to establish. That is why newly married couples always go through a period of instability. It may look to them as if marriage were not serving its purpose; but that is only because the marriage is not yet established. It takes more than a signature in a register to make a marriage; Normally, when the marriage is a love-match, the first emotional rush carries them over this tentative period, and by the time the emotions are cooling down to normal, the development of the aura is well under way, and the first quarrels end in reconciliation, not separation, because the partners to the marriage discover that they have an indefinable need of each other.

It is this fact that makes bereavement a shock, even when the marriage has been nominally unhappy and full of friction. People may laugh at the grief of widows and widowers who were notorious for doing nothing but fight with their respective spouses; but nevertheless the sense of loss may be perfectly genuine. There is an old saying that all dead husbands are good husbands; and another to the effect that a bad husband is better than no husband at all. This indicates that a woman depends upon the magnetism of her mate to a far greater extent than is realized, and that she suffers serious loss when that magnetism is withdrawn.

A male, on the other hand, is naturally a polygamous creature; he does not depend on woman's magnetism in the same way; his dependence upon marriage, as distinguished from promiscuous relations, which meet his physical need well enough, is social, in its broadest and also in its highest sense where it merges into the spiritual. He needs his home as a place of refuge from the world; and this only the marriage aura can give him. But he also needs to escape from his home at regular and frequent intervals, lest his magnetism be drawn upon unduly and the integrity of his personality impaired.

12.

The Problem of the Unpolarized

Having pointed out the importance of the exchange of magnetism between the sexes, I shall naturally be asked concerning the problem of the unmated, and therefore unpolarized. I have dealt with the psychological and physiological aspects of this problem in detail, together with their practical applications, in my book, *The Problem of Purity*, and there is therefore no occasion neither is this the place, to go into these aspects in their practical details. It may be of interest, however, to show the principles which must be taken into account in seeking a solution of this problem.

We live in an epoch of rapid changes in public opinion, and therefore in private conscience. The conditions that prevailed at the time *The Problem of Purity* was written have largely passed away. And although its practical advice is still valid, some of the problems it was designed to overcome have solved themselves. There is no longer the rigid taboo upon the discussion, or even the private study, of what the Americans call sexology. It would be difficult to find anyone nowadays who is fundamentally ignorant of the facts of life; nor, outside the ranks of the neurotic, will one find anyone who shies away from the subject in horror. It has taken its place along with such problems as sanitation and eugenics; it is one of the topics that are not usually broached at the dinner-table among those who have only just been introduced, but which can be dealt with without panic when the occasion arises. Our attitude towards sex is no longer comparable to the attitude towards ghosts of the person who has occasion to pass through the churchyard at midnight.

Experience shows that the average, healthy person of sound stock, who has had a reasonably wholesome upbringing, and is neither repressed nor stimulated in matters of sex, may have a certain amount of difficulty at the two periods of stress, puberty and the change of life, when the endocrines are temporarily out of balance, but that apart from this their physical sex-life is a self-regulating mechanism. If it is not, it is a case for the doctor, and probably quite a simple one. Much that in the old days was taken to a priest can be readily and effectually dealt with by an aperient.

The problem of non-polarization is not one that either arises or is solved on the physical plane alone. It occurs in marriage as well as out of it; and in fact, marriage breaks up on this point more often than on any other; nor is it only the childless marriages that split on this rock.

As seen in previous pages, the etheric magnetism radiated by the male is not limited in its manifestation to actual physical relations. It is concentrated there, it is true, but it is also being radiated all the time at a low potency. If therefore the unmarried woman has opportunity of comradeship and social intercourse with congenial males, she will get quite enough male magnetism to prevent her from suffering from a deficiency pathology analogous to those which occur when there is a lack of fresh fruit and green vegetables. The warping of character and conduct in the unpolarized female is just as much a deficiency disease as scurvy.

There is another factor, however, which plays a part in producing the symptoms of that condition which starts as prudery and, carried to extremes, becomes old maid's insanity. There are only three ways in which a woman can achieve independence and, consequently, the full development of her adult individuality. She must have private means; she must have adequate wage-earning capacity; or she must marry. Many pathologies which are regarded by the psychoanalysts as sex repressions are really individuality repressions, where some woman, dependent upon the whims of relatives for the means of existence, has been condemned to a narrow and thwarting life as the daughter at home. It is rare to see this type of pathology among bachelor women, even if the home of their bachelorhood be only a bed-sitting room. Be it ever so humble, and be their means never so narrow, they can at least be themselves, and their personalities are not repressed or warped. There is all the difference in the world between a thwarting by circumstances from without, and the thwarting of impulses from within by a misplaced sense of duty, or lack of courage to do the thing that is desired.

We must remember, however, that there is just as wide a range in the needs of individuals with regard to their sex nature as there is in their appetite for food. There are persons for whom celibacy is unsatisfactory, or even incompatible with health and peace of mind. There are others

who not only have no need of marriage, but would never make satisfactory
mates. Both these extremes are within the limits of normality, happiness,
and good morals provided square pegs are not driven ruthlessly into
round holes. If one of the first type marries one of the second type,
naturally there is trouble, though both might have been perfectly
satisfactory mates for persons of their own type.

It is time we gave up thinking of sex as a vice, as the Christian thinks
of it; or as a virtue, as the Hindu thinks of it, and regard it as a function.
For that is how Nature thinks of it, and at the last resort she enforces
her views. It is a function, however, which has to be exercised in relation
to the rights and needs of other persons; it can never be an end in
itself save for the heartless libertine. It is this social aspect of the sex
problem that complicates it so much, and prevents it from being a simple
problem of function, like nutrition. We shall get some salutary light on
the problem however, if we remember that there was a time when the
amount a man drank was the subject of almost as rigorous social taboo
as the purity of a woman is subject to nowadays. The teetotaller in a
regimental mess in the good old days had just as bad a time of it as
the unfortunate female who has lost her virtue. This should give us to
think and humble our spiritual pride.

Generation by generation, public opinion is coming more and more
into line with physiological fact in relation to matters of sexual morality;
and slowly but surely the law is catching up with public opinion. The
more desperate problems of marriage and celibacy are becoming rarer.
A marriage that has proved to be a mistake can be dissolved without
ruining the lives of either party, provided the financial aspect is capable
of solution. It is the throwing of a penniless, middle-aged gentlewoman
upon the unskilled labour-market that is the real divorce problem. As
far as social hardship or moral problems go, a man might keep as many
ex-homes going as he could afford. That, in fact, is what high society
does, and no one appears to be any the worse for it.

The acutest sex problems do not occur at the top of the tree, where
there is sufficient money to allow of the free play of both temperaments;
nor at the bottom, where the woman has to do her own housework
and raise her children unaided; but in between, where there is neither
enough money for freedom nor enough work for idle hands to do, and
folk have time to get into mischief and to feel sorry for themselves.

Index

Eastern Schools, 69, 74, 75, 88, 97, 101-5
ectoplasm, 84-5, 89
ego, hypertrophy of, 113
Egypt, ancient, 54, 55
electricity, 160-61
emotion,
    communication of, 129, 131
    group, 129
    psychism distorted by, 151
    source of astral energy, 84
endocrines, 103, 170
environment,
    control of 130-31, 132-5
    karmic instrument, 143-4, 145, 147
ether, reflecting, 45, 137, 138
etheric magnetism,
    nature of, 160-63
    role in sexual relationships, 164-8, 170
etheric substance, see ectoplasm
Eucharist, 58, 66
evil, 61-2, 76-80
    see also Left-hand Path
evolution, aim of, 145
exorcism, 60, 85

faith, 37
family, 163, 165
father–child relationship, 162, 163
fear, 134-5
food,
    earthing effect, 141
    sharing, 166-7
free association, 29, 30, 32, 46

gender, past life, 142
Gizeh, Great Pyramid of, 54
God, 19, 21, 93
gods, ancient, 36
Great White Lodge, 66, 83, 97
group-mind, 58-61, 116, 118
group-soul, 59, 99

healing, spiritual, 126, 156-7
Hebrew, 53
Heindel, Max, 94
higher self, 47, 68, 136-7, 138
Hindus, 102, 103
homosexuality, 83-4
honesty, 17
Horder, Sir Thomas, 95
horoscope, see astrology; planetary
    influences
humanitarianism, 88, 96-7
hypnogogics, 140

hypnotism, 73, 77-8

imagination, control of, 134-5
incense, 84
Individuality, see higher self
Initiation, 114
Inner Light, Society of, 123
Inquisition, Holy, 69
insanity, see mental instability
intuition, 28, 29

Jains, 97
Jekyll and Hyde, 67
Jesus,
    compassion, 97
    diet, comment on, 94
    ideal Initiator, 68
    Sacred Name, invocation, 61-2, 66
judgment, faulty, 144-5
Jung, C. G., 30

karma,
    acceptance, 147-8
    group, 59-60
    horoscope indication of, 40-41, 92
    initiate's approach to, 147, 148-9
    nature of, 143, 149
    problems caused by, 138-9, 144-5
    racial, 127
    relationships based on, 48, 49-50
    working out, 50, 63, 92, 126-7, 133-4,
        143-50
Kruger, President, 55
Kundalini, 81

Latin races, 104
law and order, 117
Left-hand Path,
    aims, 21, 77
    character deterioration of those on, 79-80
    descent into, 23
    domination of victim, 79, 156
    drugs, and, 77, 115
    exposure by press, 83
    hypnosis, and, 77-8
    nature of, 76
    opposing, 61-2, 66, 79-80, 117
    psychics afraid of, 88
    sex used on, 81, 82-3, 83-4
    types of followers, 76
Lemuria, 35
Levi, Eliphas, 94
logic, 36-7
Logos, 19, 115, 116